IT'S NOT FAIR!

GRACE THAT BOTH OFFENDS AND BEFRIENDS

DR GUY CHEVREAU

RIVER
PUBLISHING

River Publishing & Media Ltd
Bradbourne Stables
East Malling
Kent
ME19 6DZ
United Kingdom

info@river-publishing.co.uk

ISBN 978-1-908393-58-6
Cover design by www.spiffingcovers.com
Printed in the United Kingdom

For further information about the author visit:
www.guychevreau.com
Follow on Twitter: @ChevreauGuy

CONTENTS

DEDICATION

To Martha May—
Who promised you fair?
—*Uncle Arm*

ACKNOWLEDGEMENTS

———•———

I have never read any of Stephen King's fiction. My copy of his superb memoir, *On Writing*, is another matter. The poor thing is dog-eared, underlined in different colours, and thoroughly worked over. I trust the pages that follow are in some way worthy of his tutelage.

Well into his instruction, King counsels a writer to submit the emerging manuscript to an "Ideal Reader." This is a person who believes in you and your work, but not so much that they're unwilling to critique it. I am privileged to have several Ideal Readers, and I've tried my best to listen very carefully to their questions about the bits they didn't understand, to heed their helpful suggestions, and purge the parts they found boring. My brother Dave, Dr. Chris Shaw, and Nev Green have all played out their parts as Ideal Readers, and have each helped make this a better book. Thank you yet again.

And Kerry – among my Ideal Readers, you are, as King says, "the one I want to wow."[i] For one exquisite grace after another, my gratitude is boundless.

Notes
i. Stephen King, *On Writing*, Simon and Schuster, New York, 2000, p.220.

FOREWORD

———•———

I was very deeply moved by reading this book, *It's Not Fair*. Guy Chevreau has done a masterful job of bringing a clear sound to the subject of subjects — grace. Grace, when properly spoken of, endears us to the grace-giver. It compels us to seek him for all his beauty, wonder, and overwhelming kindness. It becomes increasingly clear that grace is an expression of the kindness that leads to repentance. As such, this wonderful gift empowers us and brings true freedom.

This book is filled with encouragement and inspiration. I found myself giving God praise from cover to cover, simply because of the beauty of his heart that is so gloriously unveiled. But it is also fair to say I was challenged. Grace does that. As a concept, grace offends only a few. It's easy to "amen" great points of the grace theology. The application of truth is what causes the most discomfort for most of us. The author's applications are brilliant, spot on, and profoundly simple. I found myself rejoicing in the grace-filled stories. But there were also a few times I cringed. Not because I sensed error. I cringed because I could see that I might not have passed that exam. In part, that's what makes a good book for me. I don't want to read only what I agree with or am practicing in a reasonably consistent fashion. I don't want to stay the same. This God-given journey called life requires that I also embrace the moments when I'm challenged. Becoming more like Jesus is always the goal. *It's Not Fair* contributes wonderfully to that end.

This book also exposes the foolishness of the thought that we can earn our salvation through good works. As the author stated so well, "as soon as we drag even a shred of merit into the equation, it's no longer Good News." The Christian walk is often crippled by self-examination, which usually results in introspection, shame and performance. This keeps us from the grace that takes us in our imperfect and messy state. When Jesus came, he fulfilled the requirements of the law and brought a grace that was overwhelmingly received by the "undeserving" and overlooked by the Pharisees.

Guy Chevreau has written a redemptive book through which the reader will find grace in each page as well as the challenge to take another look at the full effect of grace on our lives.

Bill Johnson
Bethel Church–Redding, CA
Author of *When Heaven Invades Earth* & *The Power that Changes the World.*

INTRODUCTION

—•—

I have a young god-daughter named Martha. One of our favourite outings involves a long walk down to the Quarry, a local green-space. It's where we play one of our favourite games. She and her older sister climb into their two-seater stroller and do up their little seat belts. When there's enough clear space on the broad promenade, I trot for twenty meters and aim them towards either a big tree or the bank of the river that runs beside the pavement. I give the stroller a heave as I yell with mock horror, *"Oh NO! Runaway push-chair!"* I then sprint to catch the stroller before there's a catastrophic moment.

Before you feel compelled to call Children's Services and report me, I only create the illusion of danger. The push-chair always runs out of momentum before it reaches the tree trunk the girls are aimed at, and they never really get very close to the river bank. They're never at any real risk, and they know it, because they trust me. But they love the thrill of the spill, and as soon as I've rescued them they squeal, "Again! Do it again!"

As we lurch our way along the promenade, I always find it interesting to see the looks of those who are walking towards us, but are yet outside our range of play. Some share our delight and think it all great fun. I've overheard some children say, "Daddy, do it to me!" With an elfish grin, I always apologise to these fathers.

But not everybody shares in our abandon. Given the scowls on some faces, I conclude that there are those who think Runaway Push-chair is completely irresponsible. Some show alarm at what they perceive to be imminent disaster. Not only have I put the girls at risk; these grumps feel I've violated their personal space and put them in harm's way. It's evident that they count my behaviour unacceptable, and that if they had their way we'd be banned from the Quarry forever.

The title of this book, *It's Not Fair*, suggested itself on a walk back home from the park. Martha had trotted all the way down to the Quarry. She'd had a busy time in the playground, and had worn herself out. On the return trip, she wanted the front seat of the push-chair. Martha made the point that she'd been stuck in the rear seat for the duration of our runaway games, so now it should be her turn up front. The difficulty was that her sister was already asleep in the front seat, and we didn't want to rouse her. Martha stopped on the middle of the path, crossed her arms over her chest, and with a defiant pout declared, *"It's not fair."* She was a day short of her second birthday. How, and where, does such a construct get so firmly established in a two-year old's consciousness?

Six months earlier, one of my friends asked me what I'd been working on of late. Like that great Bible phrase "make every effort to rest,"[1] my answer seemed self-contradictory because 'work' was the counterpoint to what has occupied my study and reflection. Work is what we accomplish, the exertion of our strength to perform something. Work is what we achieve. I've been working on grace, over, and over, and over again. Grace is what is done for us, what's given to us. It's what we receive.

What complicates matters is that gifts are tricky things. They can be life-giving, and restorative, and healing; but they can also be scandalous, and unsettling, and misunderstood. And like two-year old Martha, there's something deep inside each of us that expects things to be fair. Especially when we think it's our turn, and we don't get our due, we pout and pull a strop, even if we do so with adult sophistication.

Grace and mercy aren't fair. God's kindnesses toward us are undeserved. This many of us know with our heads. But few of us are so unshakeably confident in the Lord's unfailing goodness that we can giddily cry, "Again! Do it again!" Like those in the Quarry, not everybody shares that glorious abandon. Grumps abound.

Though there's no account of Jesus playing Runaway Push-chair, the Gospels do record that he, too, made some people ecstatically happy, and seriously offended others. That wouldn't matter much if his ministry was simply an innocent pastime in the park. But we're well past the age of innocence. There's a reason the Good News is good: God doesn't have a problem bringing grace to bear in the midst of our spectacular spills. In fact, as Jesus revealed the heart of God, he's quite happy for grace to associate with failure. He's pleased to cause grace to abound where it's needed most, and deserved the least. But that always upsets some folk. Jesus was the most gracious person who has ever lived, yet there were those who thought his conduct and his associations were absolutely scandalous.

Weighed in the balance, those who took offence considered themselves deserving, and were most upset because Jesus wasn't playing by their rules. Those who got happy were those who knew they didn't deserve what Jesus had to give, and were thrilled to receive his unexpected kindnesses. It is for this reason the book's subtitle reads: *Grace that both offends and befriends.*

The chapters that follow are diverse and free-ranging, but what they have in common is a foundation of grace. Grace is who God is; grace is what God does. A number of the meditations try to come to terms with passages of Scripture that are typically taken at face value, without any consideration of context. And as some will know only too well, often these texts are imposed gracelessly. To our shame, that ought to bring us up short. If the default question 'Where's grace in this?' isn't asked, whatever someone is dictating is woefully less than what Jesus came to reveal, to establish, and to impart.

When we as his church are not founded on, and growing in grace, we are no longer the inclusive, redeeming, restoring community of faith we are called to be. This is by no means a new problem. Nearly two thousand years ago, the Apostle Paul challenged the church in Rome: "Do you despise his wealth of kindness and tolerance and patience, failing to see that God's kindness is meant to lead you to repentance?"[2]

When we as Christ's Church do not freely and extravagantly demonstrate God's kindness, we're a serious sandwich short of a picnic, and inevitably, somebody gets hurt. Church ought not to hurt. We ought to heal, like Jesus did.

Notes
1. See Hebrews 4.11
2. Romans 2.4

1
COMMIT TO KINDNESS

When required, my father named himself a failed Catholic. He wouldn't go into detail. My mother was C of E, C and E – Church of England, attending at Christmas and Easter. I grew up a practicing hellion. Like my father, I won't go into detail.

In my mid-teens, I started going to a non-denominational high school youth group, Young Life. I darkened their doors because there were lots of pretty girls, and not many guys. I thought, 'I might have a chance here.' Within a few weeks, I was quite taken with the quality of their friendships. I didn't know it then, but eighteen hundred years earlier that was how Tertullian said the Romans experienced the church: "See how they love one another."[3] Genuine love is and always has been the most compelling Gospel witness.

That's what I was seeing in the youth group – their love; when I looked inside myself… it wasn't pretty. A couple of months later, I got very drunk and watched the sun set. Out loud I said, "God, if you're there, I've made a mess of my life. If you want it, you can do whatever you want with it." A few days later, my new Christian friends helped me make a little more orthodox confession of faith.

One of the guys in the youth group kept pestering us to try his church. He kept at it for two years. Just so we could shut him up, we relented, and one evening rocked up to Spring Garden Baptist Church. Most of us had never been in a church. Ever. There were about eighty of them, about eighty of us. Twenty of us had come on our motorcycles. We freaked them out.

Years later, I learned that at the end of that Sunday evening service, the pastor called an emergency elders meeting. He was very discerning, and without apology put the issue before his leaders: "We can either make a whole lot of changes very quickly, and maybe have the privilege of discipling these kids; or we can stay as we are, and kiss them goodbye."

The pastor was also a very good preacher, so we were quite keen to come back the following Sunday night. And we were impressed. They'd repainted the car park and now had designated motorcycle parking — right in front of the church. There was a new sign on the wall: "Motorcycles Only." At the end of the service, when the pastor was shaking hands at the door, he asked us, "Anyone got a spare helmet?" Off we roared, with him on the back of my bike, waving goodbye to his congregation.

Fay and Ray Binkley were elders at that church. They invited eight of us to their home for a BBQ. After we had eaten, we played penny poker. For nearly two years, we played penny poker Friday nights at Fay and Ray's. Winner bought pizza. That may seem like no big whup, so a little context is required in order to understand the magnitude of their grace towards us. Before we showed up, these folks were strict, non-card playing, big 'B' Baptists. Their willingness to meet us, to receive us, to change whatever they had to in order to incorporate us — that radical inclusivity left a deep imprint on my spirit, and defined my understanding of the Gospel.

In the next few years of my Christian walk I worked hard at memorising Scripture, and actively witnessed to my fellow university students. I was also reading philosophy, so I was used to a good argument. Scripture was my ammunition. But I gradually realised that the more Scripture I memorised, the meaner I got. Lest anyone misunderstand, it was not the Scriptures' fault. It was me, often ramming graceless truth down people's throats. Wreck after wreck I learned that you never win an argument. Not really. You can't say you've won if you're no longer in relationship with the one you've humiliated into defeat.

Ten years later, my heart had softened considerably. I was then serving a suburban Baptist congregation as their senior minister. I spent the balance of my energy trying to re-mandate and re-mission the church such that it would begin looking beyond its own four walls. Six years into my time there, an unchurched couple named Pete and Julie[4] contacted the office. They were looking for a preacher to marry them. It would be his third marriage, her second. They were willing to meet with me for some premarital counselling, and during our time together I had the privilege of leading them to the Lord.

Thereafter, they were in church most Sundays. But they couldn't go an hour without a cigarette, so while we were singing our way through the hymn sandwich, they were just outside the doors, hoovering down their smokes. And during the last verse of the last hymn, they'd walk down the isle to the front pew, and sit right in front of the pulpit. Their beautiful smiles were quite the contrast to the scowls behind them. The lingering swirl of nicotine that trailed behind Pete and Julie was not appreciated.

That wasn't all. Julie only wore provocative clothing. There were some in the church who did and didn't like her mini-skirts. After service one Sunday, an elder approached me. He didn't look happy. He rarely did. A cut-to-the-chase kind of guy, he came straight to the point. "First Baptist really isn't Pete and Julie's kind of church." I stared at the floor for a moment and then said, "You're right. It's not my kind of church either." I resigned several months later. If Pete and Julie didn't have a place, neither did I.

———•———

Let's anchor these stories in the first chapter of John's Gospel:

The Word became flesh; he made his home among us, and we saw his glory, such glory as befits the Father's only Son, full of grace and truth…. From his full store we have all received grace upon grace; for the law was given through Moses, but grace and truth came through Jesus Christ. No one has ever seen God; God's only Son, he who is nearest to the Father's heart, has made him known.[5]

Two phrases are of special note. Firstly, Jesus "made his home among us." One translation says, he "took up residence among us."[6] Another paraphrases, he "moved into the neighbourhood."[7] Religion — any religion — is oriented the other way round. We're the ones who have to make the move. In Jesus, it's God who takes the initiative. He comes to us, into our midst, where we are, wherever we are, whatever we're up to. It's rather unsettling to think that the Spirit of Jesus was just as present with Pete and Julie while they were outside the church smoking as he was inside while we were singing our hymns, but that's the Gospel.

Secondly, Jesus comes "full of grace and truth." There is a divine order to the revelation of the heart of God, and it's just as unsettling. Grace precedes truth. In Jesus, a revelation of grace goes *before* truth. Fay and Ray Binkley opened their hearts and their home to my buddies and me, and it was their kindness and care — "grace upon grace" — that earned them the right to speak truth into our teenage lives. Had they told us straight up all that was wrong with us, we would never have been seen again. There's a very sophisticated, technical theological word for the continuous and inescapable tension that holds grace and truth together — it's *messy*. Jesus came to reveal grace, truth, and the heart of God to those who have been a mess, to those whose lives are a mess, and to those who know their life is one dumb decision short of a mess.

The thing is, there is something in us that doesn't like mess. For instance, there's the story of the woman who anointed Jesus' feet with perfume and wiped her tears of devotion with her hair.[8] The NIV introduces her as "A woman who had lived a sinful life." In the REB this woman "was living" a sinful life. There's a lot of Gospel in this little bit of grammar.

In fact, it's the difference between Law and Gospel. Did this woman quit sinning, straighten her life out, get everything sorted, and then come to Jesus; or, in the midst of the mess that she'd made of things, did she come to him, and receive the love and acceptance that only he could give? The Good News is that she — and we — come limping to Jesus in the midst of our mess. That's why the divine order is grace before truth.

———•———

Let's shift things slightly. When someone gets into trouble, where do they head? To the local pub, or the local church? JR Moehringer went to the pub. In his memoir, *The Tender Bar*, these are his opening lines:

> We went there for everything we needed. We went there when thirsty, of course, and when hungry, and when dead tired. We went there when happy, to celebrate, and when sad, to sulk. We went there after weddings and funerals, for something to settle our nerves, and always for a shot of courage just before. We went there when we didn't know what we needed, hoping

someone might tell us.

We went there looking for love… or for someone who had gone missing, because sooner or later everyone turned up. Most of all we went there when we needed to be found.[9]

A quick moment of reflection: is that how you think of church? Either the church you're attending, or the one you've stopped fellowshipping with? Do you go to church for everything you need? Do you go to church when you're thirsty, hungry, or dead tired? Do you gather with your church when happy, to celebrate; when sad — hopefully not to sulk — but to be comforted? Do you go for courage? Do you gather when you don't know what you need, hoping that someone would tell you? Do you go looking for love? Most of all, do you go needing to be found?

I think that's a terrific description of what church should be. At very least, it tells us what the world needs the church to be. The embodiment of grace and truth.

———•———

However… towards the end of the Old Testament, in the little book of Zechariah, there's a rather personal question posed: "What are these wounds?" The answer is really quite desperate: "I got them in the house of my friends."[10] The number of people wounded in church is nothing short of scandalous. There would be few reading this book who do not know of folks that have been so wounded in church they've yet to return, and may never do so. They still believe in God, but do not belong to a local church fellowship. One survey group calls this segment of the population the *"De-churched,"* those who say they have a personal relationship with God, but who have stopped going to church.[11] I know a number of folks who fall — hard — in that category. I was staggered to learn — get ready for this — in England the de-churched outnumber regular church attenders two to one. There are twice as many disappointed, hurt, jaded believers as there are faithful few.

Whether or not they've stopped going to church, it's rare that someone feels wounded because another was excessively gracious towards them. It's very rare that someone laments, 'If they're kind to me one more time, I'm out of here.' What wounds is an abuse of the truth. Pause for a moment's reflection: can you recall times when you've been subjected to graceless truth — times when folks may have been right in what they were saying, but wrong in the spirit in which that truth was delivered.

Grace has to precede truth, or it's not Good News. It's the experience of grace that softens the heart, and opens the spirit, so that truth can be received. Otherwise, most of the time, we're too defensive. I learned this early in my walk. Back in 1978, I expected to marry my high school sweetheart. We'd planned an August wedding. That April, I returned from seminary, all ready to ramp up the wedding machinery, only to find myself dis-engaged. My fiancé had fallen in love with Bruce, a guy I led a youth group with. (I never did like Bruce.)

The news knocked the bottom right out of my pail. I was gutted, and I didn't recover quickly. After church, the Sunday after what was supposed to be our wedding day, one of the elders came up to me. He was my buddy's dad; he knew what had happened. What hadn't happened. He put his hand on my shoulder and said, "God causes all things to work together for good."[12] I stared at his face, then stared at my fist. I stared at his face, then stared at my fist. I decided it wasn't worth punching his lights out. What he said was true: God does cause all things to work together for good. I can testify to that. But the way he spoke that truth was graceless. It was an abuse of the truth.

Next month, September 1978, I started my second year of seminary. But I was still in quite a state, and it seemed stupid to be studying Greek and Hebrew when I couldn't read my Bible in English. During the first year of seminary, I had become good friends with my systematics professor, Dr MRB Cherry. At the end of that dark September, he and I went for a long walk on the beach. I told him I was thinking about withdrawing from seminary, and going to Europe. He listened as I poured out my pain, and my confusion, and my anger, and my disappointment.

Cherry was born and raised in Kentucky. In his gentle southern drawl, he spoke words I'll never forget: "Guy, I love you. I'll love you if you go; I'll love you if you stay. You do what you need to do. I'll be here for you when you come back; I'll be here for you if you stay. Nothing you do can change me being here for you."

Cherry's words gave me both the security and the courage to re-examine and rebuild my life. It's been the constant at every critical moment of my life. When I most needed help, what made the difference was kindness. The people that have had the greatest impact on my life have done so because they loved me. In a moment of crisis, what made the difference was that someone was present with me, listening attentively, demonstrating unconditional acceptance, bringing a revelation of the heart of God to bear on what I was facing. Graced truth.

Here's my working principle: until I've shown kindness, I haven't earned the right to speak truth. It's become my mantra: 'Commit to kindness.' That may sound a bit daft, but it doesn't take much to review my reactions, and ask myself, 'How much of the time is kindness an option? How often am I something less than kind?'

'Commit to kindness.' I try to make that the default. Just

before I rant at some idjit boy-racer who just cut me off, I try to mumble 'Commit to kindness.' Just before I get all critical and pass judgement on somebody, I try to remind myself, 'Commit to kindness.' Just before I put myself and my needs first, I'm learning to 'Commit to kindness.'

While I actively pray to know the will of God for my life, I know that it gives the Holy Spirit great delight if I ask him for the grace of excessive kindness. It seems that he gets very excited about the possibilities, and I have a growing sense that I will never know whose life I might play a part in changing.

Notes

3. *Apology, 39.7, Ante-Nicene Fathers, vol. 3,* Hendrickson Pub. Co., Peabody, Mass., 1994, p.46.
4. Their names have been changed.
5. John 1.14-18
6. NET.
7. The Message.
8. Luke 7.36-7, 1984. The 2011 revision corrected the phrase to read, "a woman who lived."
9. *The Tender Bar,* Hyperion: New York, 2006, p.1.
10. Zechariah 13.6, NIV.
11. Tearfund: "Churchgoing in the UK," 2007, p.6.
12. Romans 8.28, NASB.

2
ONLY THE DEAD GET RAISED

One of my favourite newspaper cartoons was called *Tumbleweeds*. It took its name from the main character, a rather dim-witted cowboy. In my favourite strip Tumbleweeds is downcast, and says to Ace, his best friend, "I didn't get a single Christmas present in my Easter basket." Ace says, "You dummy! You get *Christmas* presents under the *Christmas* tree. You get *Easter* eggs in your *Easter* basket." In the final panel Ace laments, "That boy's grasp of theology is pathetic."

All in, the vast majority of us are more in Tumbleweed's camp than Ace's. We don't quite have the theological grasp we should. Now, that's not an insult. It's not easy grasping hold of One whose "thoughts are higher than our thoughts, whose ways are higher than ours." That text in Isaiah 55 necessarily means that we're always going to be stretching. Add to it the Apostle Paul's great prayer in Ephesians 3, that the Lord would do "immeasurably more than all we can ask or imagine," and we have to come to terms with the fact that most of the time, we haven't got a clue.

An unlikely text may help us get a better grip, the one known as the Parable of the Pharisee and the Tax Collector.[13] But put things on pause right at the outset. The second part of the concluding verse typically eclipses the point of the parable, and so we lose its universe-cracking consequence as it sails right over our heads. The concluding verse is, in itself, profoundly true, but in this parable Jesus was teaching far more than a simple, straightforward lesson in humility. The last bit reads: "Everyone who exalts himself will be humbled; and whoever humbles himself will be exalted."[14] Again, that is true — but there's so much more here than a call to humility. This is a parable about resurrection life. And while it is great news, it's also the very unsettling declaration that the only way to life ... is death. This parable sounds the death knell of performance. Jesus taught that there is absolutely nothing any one of us can do to make ourselves right with God, and he went to great lengths to show how ridiculously absurd it is to even try.

By way of context, this parable comes near the end of a long section which the Revised English Bible gives the subheading, 'Opposition and Questioning.' Time and again, Jesus had upset the Pharisees, the religious of the day, because he was so *un*religious. He just didn't seem to understand the whole kosher construct — clean and unclean, righteous and unrighteous, judgment and mercy. He kept colouring *way* outside the lines.

Three chapters earlier, for instance, "Another time" — even "Once again" — "the tax collectors and sinners were all crowding in to listen to Jesus; and the Pharisees and the teachers of the law began murmuring their disapproval: 'This man welcomes sinners and eats with them.'"[15] In other words, 'He's runnin' with the *wrong* crowd.' By way of response, Jesus told three parables: the lost sheep, the lost coin, and the lost boys. He did so because Jesus wanted to make it clear, 'There's no such thing as "the wrong crowd."' In the next chapter, Jesus said to the Pharisees: "You are the people who impress others with your righteousness; but God sees through you; for what is considered admirable in human eyes is detestable in the sight of God."[16] Though Luke makes no editorial comment on this statement, it's safe to presume that the Pharisees didn't find themselves suddenly enamoured with Jesus. Fifteen verses after the parable of the Pharisee and the Tax Collector, Jesus told his disciples, for the third time, that he will be betrayed, killed, and that on the third day he will rise again. That's the four-sided frame, the context, in which the parable of the Pharisee and the Tax Collector is set: opposition, scandal, faith, and resurrection. And we get to choose our sides: opposition and scandal, or faith and resurrection.

Now to the parable in Luke 18. Three characters drive the story: a Pharisee, a tax collector, and God. First, the Pharisee. For this parable, you have to erase the bad rap that the Pharisees usually receive like in the verse just quoted.[17] No "white-washed tombs, hypocrites, vipers' brood." Not the Luke 18 Pharisee. He's a really nice guy. You'd like him. He's fair in all his dealings, he's faithful to his wife, and goes to all of his kids' ball games. And he's not just a good, decent bloke. He's disciplined, body, soul and spirit. He's grateful, and shows it: God gets the first ten per cent of all that he earns. You'd be thrilled to have him join the church. In fact, you'd probably elect him to leadership within the year.

Now, the second character — the tax collector. This is a guy that should give you the creeps. He's a traitor. He works for the Romans, and squeezes from his own countrymen all the dough he can extort, and does so 'legally.' He owns the biggest house in town, drives a Bentley, and flaunts his trophy wife, *and* his mistress. Sometimes at the same time.

And then there's God. I don't want to spoil the story so let's just say, he's full of surprises. Now, off we go to the Temple. The Pharisee has come to give thanks: as far as he's concerned, life's good; he's good; he's done good. In contrast, the tax collector falls flat on his face, because quite literally he knows he hasn't a hope in hell. And what does God do? Nothing — absolutely nothing — for the Pharisee.

That ought to rock our religious worlds. It did when Jesus first told this story. It's the whole point of the parable, and the Gospel, because God is in the redemption business. He restores. That's who he is; that's what he does. And because the Pharisee figures he's fine just as he is, there's nothing for God to do.

In contrast, the tax collector knows he's made a right mess of things. Like the Flim-flam Man, he has an M.B.S., a C.S., and a D.D. — Master of Back-Stabbing, Cork-Screwing and Dirty-Dealing. There isn't a commandment he hasn't broken. But notice: there's no blaming, no bargaining, no pathetic attempt at self-justification. He simply pleads for mercy. And because the tax collector rests his case on a life that God can only redeem, there is acquittal. There is restoration. There is resurrection life.

So far so good. I doubt anybody's too fussed. Now let's look at things with a wide-angle lens. The fact is both men, the Pharisee and the tax collector, are dead in their sins. The Apostle Paul put it this way: "All have sinned, and fall short of the glory of God."[18] And the wages of sin is death. For all, each and everyone of us. Whether we know it or not. Whether we acknowledge it or not.

The Good News — the message of resurrection life — is that God raises the dead. But that's the point of this parable: he *only* raises the dead. Because the Pharisee was so busy trying to impress God with his accomplishments, he failed to notice that God isn't keeping count. At all. The Pharisee was so impressed with himself he missed the fact that since Jesus showed up, there's only one game in town — Mercy. And there's only one rule to the game: Mercy triumphs over judgment.

Well, if you've tracked with me so far, there's a good chance you've concluded that the Pharisee is a fool. Mercy is on offer, and he's crazy enough to try to impress God with his performance. Correct. He is a fool. But best not get smug. There's something yet of the fool in each of us. There's something in each of us that also tries to impress with our performance and accomplishments. And the scandal of unconditional mercy unhinges us.

Allow me to extrapolate — to stretch the story. Imagine, for a moment, that this parable is a retelling of what we call the parable of the prodigal son in Luke 15, only thirty years later. The prodigal son has come home from squandering his father's fortune on wine, women and song, they've celebrated his return — the robe, the ring, the fatted calf — the whole enchilada; he's then gone off to university, trained as a chartered accountant, and become a very 'successful' tax collector — a Master at Back-Stabbing, Cork-Screwing and Dirty-Dealing — the tax collector in the Luke 18 parable. Imagine, for a moment, that the duty-driven elder brother in Luke 15 spends the thirty years devoting himself to the study of the Law, and becomes the squeaky-clean Pharisee in the second parable. Do you see the congruity, the similarity? Do you see that neither the duty-bound elder brother nor the Pharisee have a clue about either the heart of God or resurrection life? And are you ok with the prodigal son — now a dirty-dealing tax collector — once again, thirty years later, throwing himself on the mercies of God, and receiving the whole enchilada of unbounded forgiveness, all over again?

I know that some of you may feel I'm reading too much into things, so we'll keep things immediate. Imagine that the Luke 18 tax collector goes home from Temple, having had this glorious experience of unconditional, unmerited forgiveness. He's giddy in the knowledge that his slate has been wiped clean. He's a new man! He has a do-over! He can't stop singing *"O—happy day; o happy day-ay-ay..."*

And one week later, he returns to Temple — with nothing in his life reformed. He's had another full and busy week of extortion, wenching, and single malt whisky. The Macallan, 18 year-old, his favourite. But here he is, back in Temple, crying at the altar, beating his breast, and pleading for mercy. Ready? Just as he has not changed his ways, neither has God.

This creep goes home, acquitted, again, just like he did last week. Unconditional, unmerited forgiveness are his, again. You ok with that? For most of us, we suddenly feel the need to yak up a fur ball. The bounder can't keep getting away with it, can he?

Can we?

We're not the only ones having trouble here. What to do with often-sinning believers has always been a problem. Just a little more than a hundred years after Christ died, in a treatise called *The Shepherd of Hermas*, a hard line was drawn: "Repentance for the righteous has its limits."[19] One hundred years after that, things had become even crustier: "There is no further pardon for sinning after you have begun to know God."[20] While completely understandable, such a graceless posture completely misses the Gospel. And we'd all fall short. I know I'm able to trace at least a few habitual sins that keep me entangled, and for which I plead ongoing, ever-repeated forgiveness, sometimes on a weekly basis. If you're not aware of any similar entanglement dear reader, may I suggest you pray about the sin of indifference.

——•——

All of this leaves most of us feeling like the rug is being pulled from underneath our feet. We feel all base over apex, so try it another way. What if the tax collector goes back to Temple the following week after trying really hard to live as a new man. He's cut back fifteen per cent on the graft; he only goes out wenching twice, and he's drinking blended Scotch. But wait; God wasn't impressed with the Pharisee's righteousness. Why would he commend the tax collector for sinning just a little bit less?

Perhaps you're finding it difficult to breathe again. Isn't there something to be said for his good intentions? Doesn't he get some credit for trying to reform his life? Oops. The point of the parable is that he confessed that he was dead, not that in spite of his behaviour he wanted to be a good person.

Most of us have trouble grasping the Good News that Jesus only raises the dead. And some of you are not happy Easter bunnies right now. I've been around the block often enough to anticipate the questions: Is there no distinction to be made? Isn't the Pharisee somehow a better person, isn't he somehow 'further along' than the tax collector? What about 'proving repentance by the fruit one bears'?[21] Doesn't the Pharisee get any credit for his life-long commitment to righteousness and godly living? Don't we?

Asking those questions makes exactly the same mistake the Pharisee made: 'Thank you, God, that I am not like the rest of mankind — greedy, dishonest, adulterous — or for that matter — like the guy sitting next to me.'[22] It misses the whole Gospel point. Because as soon as we drag even a shred of merit into the equation, it's no longer Good News. As soon as we factor into the equation what we've done — or not done — it is no longer resurrection life. It's religion. But Christian faith is not religion. It is the glorious declaration of the end of religion.

The word 'religion' comes from the Latin word *ligare*, 'to bind.' Religion is about 'rules,' what we've tried to do to get right with

God: what to believe, how to behave, what to do, what not to do. Religion says, 'Play this game well, and you win.' The Good News is that resurrection life isn't about binding — think of the story of the raising of the dead man, Lazarus. What did Jesus say once Lazarus came out of the tomb? "Loose him; let him go."[23]

Some of you are still working on your religious fur ball. Back way up, to the Ten Commandments.[24] How do they start? If you answer, "You shall have no other gods before me," that's the first commandment. The following do's and don't's define the life that God expects of his people, right? 'Keep the Sabbath holy; honour your father and mother; do not commit murder; do not commit adultery; do not steal....'

There's a frame around the Ten Commandments, and unless we put them in that frame, we'll miss God's heart. Here it is: "I am the Lord your God who brought you out of Egypt, out of the land of slavery."[25] In other words, 'I am the Lord of freedom; I've set you free. Now, here are ten ways to stay free.' The Ten Commandments are not a list of what God expects us sorry lot to live up to. They are ten ways for us to live the life of freedom God set us free to live.

Make it New Testament. At the start of his public ministry Jesus said, "The Kingdom of God is upon you. Repent, and believe the Gospel."[26] Repentance is our response to the mercy and kindness of God. It is not that which makes us acceptable to God. He loves and accepts us *before* we respond. He loves and accepts us regardless of our response. The word 'repentance' literally means changing the way we think. This change of mind enables us to then change the way we live, and that in turn enables us to appropriate heaven's blessings. Repentance enables us to live out of the fullness of God's mercies. Like living out of the Ten

Commandments, repentance enables us to live free, and full, and blessed. If we don't repent, we forfeit the grace that could be ours. It's us saying 'No' to the gifts that are on offer.

Consider the story of the woman caught in adultery. In keeping with the Law, the Pharisees wanted to stone her to death. Jesus said, "Let whichever of you is free from sin throw the first stone at her."[27] The gathered crowd came under conviction, and split. Jesus said to the woman, "Has no one condemned you? Neither do I. Go; do not sin again." Undeserved forgiveness was hers. Unconditional mercy, not judgment.

Forgiveness and mercy were not conditional on her sinless future — Jesus did not say, "*If* you straighten up and fly right, *then* you'll be forgiven this heinous sin, *but just this once.*" When Jesus said, "Go and sin no more," he was not binding her forgiveness to her sanctification: "*If* you live a holy and righteous life, *then* I'll forgive you." Rather, he was inviting her to the blessings of a redeemed and transformed life. Her 'Yes' to that invitation enabled her to receive all the grace that Jesus had to give.

This makes such a huge difference. Life is good. It's God's idea, and he's good. When life is lived according to God's designs, it's terrific. It's beautiful, because he's beautiful. Even in this fallen world, we touch something of the goodness and the beauty God intends when we live as he hopes we will live.

However. But. Nevertheless. In spite of all that, the dismal truth is that we don't live well. If the human race could have sorted itself by choosing to pursue goodness and beauty, it would have done so long ago. We're not stupid, and there have been hundreds of wise men and women who've tried to teach us — Socrates, Augustine, … Joyce Meyer?

But as bizarre as it sounds, we cannot be saved by living decently. We just don't live well enough to do get the job done.

Our best goodness is a flawed goodness. I'll make it personal. I love my kids — Graham and Caitlin — fiercely. I've tried to nurture them, and bless them, and raise them to be the best they can be. And I've bought them the inner healing books. I've told them I tried my best, and where I've failed them, my hope is that they will freely forgive me.

We all want to be good, and loving, and nurturing, don't we? (Anybody out there genuinely *want* to be a bounder?) Despite our best intentions, we all miss the mark. Our goodness, and love, and nurture isn't enough to eradicate the selfishness and the woundedness that corrupts life.

———•———

Nearly done, and so a test question: What is the opposite of sin? Most of us are inclined to answer, 'Righteousness.' But it's not. The opposite of sin is faith. The Apostle Paul contended: "Everything that does not come from faith is sin."[28] How kind of God to make it so, because very few of us have all the issues of performance settled and sorted. *"Am I good enough?" "Do I make the grade?" "Must try harder."* We will never be truly free until we are dead to the whole business of measuring up. Righteousness — measuring up — is not a viable option for us. We cannot achieve our own righteousness. Instead, we're called to trust in Jesus. To put our faith in him who is the resurrection and the life, the One who raises... the dead. All that has needed to be done has been done — by him.

For those who are still hung up on performance, let it BE all about performance — but it's HIS, not yours. If you'd like a $57 theological concept for all of this, it's called imputed righteousness. An exchanged life. 'His life for yours.' 'All that he is, for all that you are.' And it all hinges on death. His death, and yours. Because an exchanged life also means 'Your life for his.' 'All that you are, for all that he is.'

Only the dead get raised, and death is death. Not partly dead, not mostly dead. All dead. One of the things this means is that we have to die to our own understanding, of ourselves, of life, and how we think it should unfold, in order to rise to a further revelation of the unconditional, unmerited goodness of God. Now, *that* death is not morbid, because our Heavenly Father's faithfulness is greater than our hopes and our longings.

Take a deep breath. Open your heart, and hear, again, the Good News of resurrection life: there is nothing, absolutely nothing, that we can do to make God love us any less than he does right now. And there's nothing, absolutely nothing, that we can do to make God love us any more than he does right now. Neither our failures, regrets and compromises nor our successes, accomplishments or our disciplines play into the equation whatsoever.

Repeat after me, "Lord, have mercy...."

Notes
13. Luke 18.9-14
14. Verse 14b
15. Luke 15.2, NIV.
16. Luke 16.15
17. Luke 16.15
18. Romans 3.23, NIV.
19. Book I, Vision II, Chapter II.
20. Cyprian, On the Dress of Virgins, Chapter II.
21. See Luke 3.8. Note that this was required by John the Baptist, not Jesus.
22. See Luke 18.11
23. John 11.44
24. Exodus 20
25. Exodus 20.2
26. Mark 1.15
27. John 8.7
28. Romans 14.23, NIV.

3
MESSY GRACE

I have another favourite cartoon. It's of a man pointing at his cat, who is sitting beside its litter box. The caption reads: *"NEVER, EVER, think outside the box."* Just as most of us expect things to be fair, so many of us like things tidy. We want to keep the mess inside the box, thank you very much. That's fine when it comes to cats.

Church, however, ought to be a different matter. The vast majority of the churches I've visited would like to grow. Not all, but most would like to be bigger than they are. As the first church did, they'd like to be able to say, 'Day by day, the Lord has added to our numbers.'[29] Few realise that if the Lord added to their numbers day by day, it wouldn't take very long at all for church as they know it to look very different. Those whom the Lord added to the first church "were being saved."[30] As one of my friends astutely observed, "being saved" is very different from "completely saved and sorted."

To keep this from being armchair theology, ask yourself a simple question: at the end of a service at your church, is it safe to leave your phone or iPad on your chair when you go for coffee? Do you expect them to be there on your return? I know of churches where you don't leave anything lying around. I've been in churches where twenty per cent of the gathered are off the streets, men and women who, if they're not too sick to steal, will.

Instead of freaking out, try this: how about the Lord adding two new people per week, a hundred new people in a year? Could you get your head around that? A hundred new people joined to your church family next year? Try asking it another way. Would you like it if the lost, the lonely, the troubled and the broken found a home in your midst? That they came into a loving relationship with Jesus, came to know him as Saviour, Lord, best friend, and your church as their church family?

If so... let's pretend. But first the disclaimer: "*The characters and incidents portrayed are fictitious, and any similarity to actual persons, either living or dead, is entirely coincidental and unintentional.*"

Let's say that Sara has a colleague at work named Susie. She invites her to an introductory Alpha dinner. Susie enjoys herself, and comes out to the weekly meetings that follow. On week five, Susie gives her life to Jesus. Wonderful! On the Away Weekend she has a powerful encounter with the Holy Spirit. Glory! She becomes a regular at church, and she's joined a home group. Hallelujah!

Over the months that follow her boyfriend, Bill, sees a noticeable joy and freedom growing in her. He even likes it when she prays for him at night. Bill says he feels 'centred.' (By the way, Bill and Susie have been living together for two years.) And Susie? She's all excited. She wants to be baptised. An invitation was extended at church, and it got her thinking.

Now would be a great time to ask, 'Where's grace in this?' Instead, when Susie tells her home group about her desire there is a sucking of teeth and a shaking of heads. Her home group leader,

Fred, is the one to break the news: "We're very sorry Susie; you can't be baptised as long as you're living with your boyfriend."

There it is, the hard line: she's "living in sin." Not only that, in cohabiting, she's told she's committing "wilful, habitual sin." Let's pause for a quick question: how do you think boyfriend Bill is going to feel about this when Susie comes home in tears? Remember, he's started to open up. There are pretty good odds that his reaction will be something along the lines, "Just as I thought — those arrogant, judgmental hypocrites." With a few more adjectives.

Susie is gutted. It takes a week, but she makes an appointment to meet with her pastor. She tells him what's happened, and says she's been reading her Bible. She's confused. She opens to the Gospel of Matthew and starts reading:

Do not judge, and you will not be judged. For as you judge others, so you will yourselves be judged, and whatever measure you deal out to others will be dealt to you. Why do you look at the speck of sawdust in your brother's eye, with never a thought for the plank in your own?... First take the plank out of your own eye, and then you will see clearly to take the speck out of your brother's.[31]

She looks up at her pastor, and points to her Bible. "Red letters. The words of Jesus." Susie takes a deep breath. "Fred, my home group leader, he's at least sixty pounds overweight; Fiona, his wife, is a chronic shopper. Wikipedia says those are two of the seven deadly sins — gluttony and greed, and that they're lust based — 'I want it, and I want it now.' Isn't his gluttony, and her greed, 'wilful, habitual sin?' They were baptised, years ago. Why, exactly, am I getting singled out here?"

———•———

How comfortable are you 'out of the box'? It's messy. Really messy. But know this: we won't see very many unchurched people in our midst unless and until we're ready and willing to deal with the mess. Flip the idea on its head; the mess of life requires the Spirit's supernatural influence. That's what makes church, church. Law we can manage all on our own. Rules, regulations, right/wrong, in/out, that all comes pretty easily to most of us. Grace requires the Spirit's influence on our lives, and God purposes the grace that we've received to then be reflected in the way we deal with … *mess*.

———•———

This is both the heartbeat and the life-blood of Pentecost, and the outpouring of God's Spirit on the first church. To explain things, the Apostle Peter quoted the prophecy from Joel 2, when the Spirit will be poured out on all flesh, male and female, young and old, servant and free, an almost poetic declaration that all of the social barriers will be broken down. Peter concluded his sermon with the radically inclusive punch-line: "Everyone who calls on the name of the Lord will be saved."[32]

As the story goes in the early chapters of Acts, the disciples stayed in and around Jerusalem, and spoke within the Jewish household of faith. They stayed within the box. But it wasn't long before the church suffered violent persecution, and the disciples were scattered. They were kicked out of the box. Out to Judea and Samaria. They were no longer living amongst 'people of the Law.' Now they were forced to mix with the Gentiles, the 'Law-less,' if you will.

If you've grown up in something of a cosmopolitan city, you won't be able to understand the magnitude of what this means unless you think of apartheid in South Africa, or segregation in Jackson Mississippi and Birmingham Alabama back in the sixties. Think, *"Whites only."* Think, *"We don't mix with your kind, boy."* There is deep-seated, born in the blood, right to the bone, hard-core prejudice. Jew, and Gentile. Think Middle East today, Palestinian Jew, and Palestinian Arab. Not happy neighbours. Nobody's planning a street BBQ any time soon.

The Apostle Peter then had a dream, a bad dream. Actually, it's a recurring nightmare that he had three times. In it, he saw unclean animals, and he's supposed to kill and eat them. This is all *very* wrong. Good Jewish boy that he is, he cried out, 'No Lord! It's not kosher!' Yet a voice from heaven responded: "Do not call anything impure that God has made clean."[33]

About the same time, a Gentile named Cornelius had an angelic visitation, and was told to send for Peter. The Spirit had already prepared Peter, telling him he's not to hesitate to go to see him. When he arrived Peter said, 'It is against our law for a Jew (like me) to associate with or visit a Gentile (like you). But God has shown me that I should not call anyone impure or unclean.'[34] He then cracked the universe when he said, "I now understand how true it is that God has no favourites."[35] (You might check to see if you have that last line underlined in your Bible.)

In terms of the mission and history of the Church, this is a massive shift. Ministry moves from the Jews in Jerusalem, to the Gentiles and the uttermost parts of the world — definitely out of the box. And that created problems, all manner of problems for the early church. One of the biggest was, do the lawless have to conform to Jewish religious practice? It caused such division that a special meeting was called, the "Jerusalem Council." There was one issue on the agenda: 'What are we gonna do with all this mess?' It was a really big deal. As it's recorded, there was "sharp dispute and debate." Other translations aren't as understated. The REB says there was "fierce dissension and controversy."[36]

After considerable wrangling the Apostle Peter stood up and said, 'Let's get serious guys. We can't keep the Law, never have done, never will. Why should we expect them to?' He then concluded:

> God, who knows the heart, showed that he accepted them by giving the Holy Spirit to them, just as he did to us. He did not discriminate between us and them, for he purified their hearts by faith. Now then, why do you try to test God by putting on the necks of Gentiles a yoke that neither we nor our ancestors have been able to bear? No! We believe it is through the grace of our Lord Jesus that we are saved, just as they are.[37]

The Apostle James then hammered it home in case there was still any confusion: "We should not make it difficult for the Gentiles who are turning to God."[38] Oh, that it should be so.

———•———

Back to Susie, and her desire to be baptised. Grace is messy, but not sloppy. Grace is not *laissez faire*, "Whatever you want… as long as it feels good, do it." That is not grace. The Apostle Paul said "For anyone united to Christ, there is a new creation: the old order has gone; a new order has already begun."[39] The "old" is that which needs redeeming, restoring, renewing. The "old" is the broken, wounded, distorted legacy of our lives. The "new" is the fullness of blessing that our Heavenly Father purposes for our lives in Christ. The graced "re-creation."

What if her wise and gracious pastor tried to discern how the

Spirit was at work in Susie's life? That's his default — not defect — the default: the assurance that God *is* at work in Susie's life. What if her pastor tried to discern how Susie's loving Heavenly Father was drawing her unto himself? What if her pastor tried to discern how her church could help nurture her relationship with Jesus — and Bill, convinced that God does indeed want a relationship with her and with Bill, unto redemption and the fullness of blessing for their lives?

What if her pastor asks Susie, "Been to a wedding lately?" She nods, so he says, "A wedding is about commitment, right? A formal giving of self …to the other. A man and a woman make covenant promises of faithfulness and fidelity. 'To you and no other.' Same in baptism. Is that what you want? Jesus is faithfully committed to you; do you want to make that kind of commitment to him?" Susie nods. That's what she wants. Her pastor smiles. "That's wonderful. What do you think your boyfriend will say if you told him that? Think he'd come to your baptismal service?" She nods again, and her pastor then asks, "Susie, do you have any sense of what the Holy Spirit is stirring in terms of your relationship with Bill? Anything about commitment?"

———•———

Some of you reading this may be upset because I've made a big mess outside your box. Susie is committing wilful, habitual sin. Steady now. Do we really want to go down that road? What about gluttony? What about greed? What about anxiety, or fear, or hopelessness? How about anger? Control? How about good old-fashioned sloth? Anybody struggle with any of those issues on an ongoing, wilful, habitual basis?

'Living in sin.' If we take that line, we have to first ask after sin in our own lives. And remember the stark, unambiguous words of Jesus, "Judge not." It is not ours to judge because the Good

News is that in heaven there are only forgiven sinners. That's the only thing on their resumes. There's nothing of their commitment or achievements, nothing of their selfless service, nothing of their dedicated devotion. If we introduce even a shred of merit, we completely mangle the Gospel. All of heaven is only filled with flops and failures; the lost, the loose, and the losers. Every single person in heaven was dead in their sins, but raised up in Christ who died, so that they might live.

It's the same with hell, too. In hell, there are only forgiven sinners. That's the only thing on their resumes. There's no record of their wickedness, their perversions, or their godlessness. The fundamental difference between heaven and hell is that in heaven, forgiveness is accepted and kept in circulation. In hell, it is rejected, and forfeited. The Episcopal priest Robert Capon put it this way:

> Hell is only populated by those insisting on a perpetual rejection of God's perpetual gift. It is an eternal struggle to escape from the grip of love that will never let go…. Nobody goes to hell because he has a rotten track record in the world — any more than anyone goes to heaven because he had a good one. We are judged by what Jesus did for us on the cross…. Hell is just a [gracious] courtesy for those who insist they want no part of forgiveness.[40]

Back to Pentecost, and the outpouring of God's Spirit on all flesh, with all of the special effects: mighty rushing wind, tongues of fire, gifts and fruit of the Spirit, and the supernatural growth of the Church. Yes, Amen, Glory Hallelujah!! But they're the outward signs. The real miracle of Pentecost happens in the heart. The Holy Spirit reveals to our hearts the scandal of grace; he delivers us from judgmentalism, and breaks down the dividing walls of 'us and them.'

Most churches need to have a good look around. As a visiting preacher in the West, I usually stand before a pretty pasty looking bunch. What of race? Of colour? Should you feel sufficiently enlightened that that's not an issue — how about nationality? How welcome and included are the Poles? The Romanians? The Bulgarians? How about ethnicity — gypsies, for instance?

What about tattoos? Piercings? Alternative hair colour? If you're ok with all of that, what about navy blue business suits? Any prejudice against lawyers and hedge fund managers? How about golfers? Or muslims? Or satanists? Is it settled in your heart that Jesus really loves golfers, and muslims, and satanists?

There's a bottom line here: God loves the lost way too much to draw 'them' to a judgmental church. To a church that still thinks, "Us ... and 'them.'"

Notes

29. See Acts 2.47
30. Acts 2.47, NIV.
31. Matthew 7.1-5
32. Acts 2.21, NIV.
33. Acts 10.15, NIV.
34. Acts 10.28, paraphrase.
35. Acts 10.34
36. Acts 15.2
37. Acts 15.8-11, NIV.
38. Acts 15.19, NIV.
39. 2 Corinthians 5.17
40. *Kingdom, Grace, Judgment*, Eerdmans, Grand Rapids, 2002, pgs. 117 and 132.

4

THE SECRET OF THE KINGDOM

Over the last seven years, I haven't been able to preach much on a regular basis. It's been hard, even painful by times. I love to preach. I believe it's what I was made and meant to do. I believe that preaching is also both a gift and a calling, and while I'm convinced that as the Apostle Paul said, the "gracious gifts of God and his calling are irrevocable,"[41] I've concluded that in this season God wasn't calling me anywhere in particular. In this interim period, therefore, I've spent considerable time and energy gutting and renovating several houses. I take the following words to be wise counsel: "Whatever task lies to your hand, do it with might,"[42] so I've tried my best to glorify God by making beautiful spaces out of run-down, shabby and poorly designed houses. It's been challenging, to say the least. For instance, at the end of a long, hard day, most of which I spent on my knees laying ceramic tile, I looked up to the heavens, and just in case anybody was confused, I mumbled out loud, "This is not my calling."

In my prayer time the next morning, it took considerable effort to turn my grump around and correct myself, because renovations have been my calling in this season, while I wait. I've had to work hard at waiting. At times it's been exhausting, even more shattering than laying ceramic tile.

And it's often been hard to go to church. It's been hard to find a good church, a healthy church. Hard, for several reasons. The biggest stumbling block is that there's a lot of blather out there in Jesus' name. 'Waffle' is defined as 'foolish talk without purpose.' That's bad enough. 'Blather' is 'long-winded talk with no real substance.' And in a preach, blather doesn't heal. Blather doesn't bring release. Blather doesn't bless. It doesn't build. It doesn't call, or draw or empower.

For example, one Sunday, the preacher began his sermon with a question: "What is God's number-one call on your life, his highest, greatest purpose for you?" I thought that was a good question, and got all hopeful. After a pregnant pause for effect, he answered his own question and shouted, "Holiness!"

He jabbed his index finger into his open Bible and began quoting: "Who may ascend the mountain of the Lord? Who may stand in his holy place? The one who has clean hands and a pure heart."[43] What followed was a forty-minute rant in an attempt to convince us that we were a pretty sorry lot that weren't measuring up by half.

The next Sunday he was gnawing on the same bone. After a stern review of his previous message he growled, "God won't bless unrighteousness!" His text featured the destruction that came upon Israel because of the sin of Achan.[44] The message was titled, "Sin in the camp." Both Sunday messages vexed me such that during the second preach, it was either use my Bic pen to perform a frontal lobotomy on myself, or turn to one of the parables of Jesus for comfort. It was a text I'd been meditating on, and I figured I might as well work on something that would edify — at least myself. The text reads:

To you the secret of the kingdom of God has been given; but

to those who are outside, everything comes by way of parables, so that (as Scripture says) 'they may look and look, but see nothing; they may listen and listen, but understand nothing; otherwise they might turn to God and be forgiven.'[45]

I concede that it's a strange text, but from my reading of church history and theology, it stands as telling commentary on how much we have misunderstood, misinterpreted, and misconstrued. That last word, 'misconstrued,' might be outside some vocabularies. It shares the same root as the word 'construction.' To misconstrue is to 'build wonky,' and that explains a lot of church history.

—————•—————

When I'm engrossed in a novel, I'm rarely tempted to sneak a peak at the end of the book to know how it finishes up. The Scriptures are a different matter. I often look to the last chapters to remind myself that, as Anne Lamott says, "love bats last." The Apostle John gave us a picture of what the final innings look like: "I saw a new heaven and a new earth... the Holy City, new Jerusalem, coming down out of heaven from God, made ready like a bride adorned for her husband."[46]

"Coming down out of heaven from God." Down — from heaven to earth. From God — this recreation is his initiative, and his work, not ours. For all eternity, God's will and purpose is graced restoration, redemption, and perfection, unto the most intimate of relationship.

This is the Gospel counter-point to Psalm 24.4 and the preacher's call to holiness and righteousness. The question, "Who may ascend?" puts the focus on our efforts, and our works. But that misconstrues the Gospel. It adds something to the sufficiency of Christ's atoning sacrifice. The preacher missed it by a covenant. This is precisely what the Apostle Paul was at pains to convey about the message of the cross:

> No place is left for any human pride in the presence of God. By God's act you are in Christ Jesus; God has made him our wisdom, and in him we have our righteousness, our holiness, our liberation. Therefore, in the words of Scripture, 'If anyone must boast, let him boast in the Lord.'[47]

The balance of the Old Testament makes it clear that if we are not holy, not righteous, we are under judgment. That's true. But it's not Good News. It's not the secret of the Kingdom. If the focus is still on our holiness and righteousness, we "understand nothing."[48] We've completely misunderstood what John declared in his Gospel: "It was not to judge the world that God sent his Son into the world, but that through him the world might be saved."[49]

As I write this, outside my window there shines a bright, beautiful rainbow. We get a lot of rainbows in North Wales; Welsh sunshine is light drizzle. In the early chapters of the Book of Genesis there is the account of the flood, and God's judgment on the violence of mankind.[50] Things had become so seriously misconstrued, the Lord trashed the prototype and started all over. God then made this promise to Noah: "For all generations to come, this is the sign which I am giving of the covenant between myself and you and all living creatures with you..."[51] That promised sign was a rainbow.

In Bible times, a bow, as in 'bow and arrow,' was a weapon of death. In holy war it was used to eradicate unrighteousness. Instead of pointing it at us, God turned it skyward... at himself, for "It was our afflictions that he was bearing, our pain he endured.... He was pierced for our transgressions, crushed for our iniquities; the chastisement he bore restored us to health, and by his wounds we are healed."[52] The rainbow foretells the mysteries of the cross, and the redemption, restoration, and unconditional acceptance that is ours in Christ.

In the Gospels, Jesus said to his disciples, "To you the secret of the kingdom of God has been given."[53] It's a definitive statement, one that qualifies the parable that he had just told, the Parable of the Sower. As it's recorded in the Gospels, the sower was the first parable Jesus taught. It's also one of the longest, and one of the few upon which Jesus himself commented. It seems he did so because it is also the parable that calibrated all the others, hence his question: "Do you not understand this parable? How then are you to understand any parable?"[54] It's a warning: if we misconstrue the sower, our interpretation of the other kingdom parables will also be skewed.

Given the simplicity of the parable, it would be easy to conclude that the disciples were pretty thick if they didn't get it. The explanation Jesus gave seems to belabour the obvious. How can they, and we, "see nothing, understand nothing" and fail to "turn to God and be forgiven."[55]

Heeding the warning, it's best to go slowly here. "The sower sows the word."[56] (In Matthew, "the word that tells of the kingdom.") Then it's different soils, and "they hear, but…" The footpath types hear, but Satan steals away what has been sown. The rocky types hear, but trouble and trial bring compromise. The weedy types hear, but worldly cares choke the word. Some, however, are good soil and bear fruit. No buts. They "accept the word when they hear it." "They hear the word and understand it."[57]

At this point, most preaching now shifts and the question is asked, 'What kind of soil are you? How are you responding to the word of God? What are you doing with the seed that has been planted in your life? Will you be fertile soil and bear fruit for Jesus?'

The trouble is those questions make it all about us — soil, not seed. And that ought to be unsettling, because any honest assessment of our shortcomings reads like the tediously repeated teachers' comments on my school report cards: "Guy consistently fails to apply himself." "Can do better." There's no secret in any of that, and there's no revelation about the kingdom. There's also no turning to God for forgiveness, because the mystery of the kingdom is not about soil sampling.

Matthew, Mark and Luke all record the parable of the sower. The parable is missing in John. But only sort of. John was the last to write, perhaps as much as thirty years after the other three. Even in those thirty years, might things have been misconstrued, and might John have tried to take this lead, well-known, well-worked parable, and bring some reflection, some re-definition, some mid-course correction to bear?

The parable opens with these words: "A sower went out to sow." The interpretation opens, "The sower sows the word." And John said, "In the beginning the Word already was. The Word was in God's presence, and what God was, the Word was. He was with God at the beginning, and through him all things came to be; without him no created thing came into being. In him was life...."[58]

Watch what changes if it's the Father who is the sower, and as John declared, Jesus is the Word; if he is the secret of the kingdom, and that the parable is about kingdom seed, not kingdom soil. Everything changes if "hearing the word" is not so much hearing *about* Jesus, but hearing him — here, now — speaking, calling, revealing the kingdom. To the religious of the day Jesus said,

His voice you have never heard, his form you have never seen; his word has found no home in you, because you do not believe the one whom he sent. You study the Scriptures diligently, supposing that in them you have life; their testimony points to me, yet you refuse to come to me to receive that life.[59]

What, exactly, changes? The religious of the day, and any day, expect God to bless their righteousness. They expect certain privilege. They've given themselves to God; they expect him to give himself to them. And while we're at it, the religious expect God's punishment on the unrighteous.

Yet the sower flings seed about extravagantly, even carelessly. Whether it's the demonised or the worldly, the fearful or the fruitful — every human being irrespective of their condition or their response — the word of God comes to us all. Every single one of us. The seed, the secret that Jesus reveals is this: because of God's unbounded goodness, the kingdom is everywhere, always, and for all — not just in some places, at some times, for some people. In Matthew's Gospel, the parable after the Sower is the Parable of the Weeds. The main character is a farmer who sows good seed in a big field. Jesus said it's "the world." But the enemy comes along and sows bad seed in the midst of it all. Nevertheless, good seed grows and is harvested. In a following parable about the yeast, the whole loaf gets leavened. In the parable of the net, every kind of fish gets caught. John says, "God so loved the world...."

Most of us "look and look, but see nothing; we listen, but understand nothing."[60] All of this goes right over our heads, and we don't understand why, by the end of the telling of all these parables, the people have had more than enough. They turn against Jesus; literally, they are scandalised — over his teaching.[61] Why?

This radical inclusivity, this transcendence, that Jesus revealed offended their understanding of God's exclusive call. They counted themselves good soil, and this parable unsettled all that they knew of clean and unclean, chosen and unchosen, holy and unholy, righteous and unrighteous. Jesus effectively challenged their entire religious system. They worked so very hard to make sure that they were worthy of inclusion, and at the same time, worked hard to keep the wrong people out. As good soil, they'd come to know a certain privilege that they didn't particularly want to share.

It's there in the parable of the sower. There's no specific reference to Israel, no reference to Jewish soil, and no special favour for a chosen people. Quite the contrary: seed that was so carelessly flung about could get flung on the Gentiles, the unclean, the unwashed. The seed might bear fruit in them, and... there's no promise that the religious will yield much of anything.

There's more, or better, less. There's the paradox of power. The word secret, as in "the secret of the kingdom," is *mysterion* in Greek. Translated literally, it is the mystery of the kingdom. Two thousand years ago, the expectations of Messiah were well established: the Son of David would yet again establish God's reign and rule over the heathen nations. He would rule with might, leading the armies of God to drive out the unrighteousness and the infidel. Yet Jesus talked about seed. Tiny, insignificant, weeny seed. Seed that disappears, and then dies. And Jesus said that some of that seed, in good soil, yields thirty, sixty, a hundred fold.

Those of us city folks completely miss what he was saying there. In his day, a farmer was very pleased with a seven per cent yield. That would be considered a good harvest. Kingdom yield is at least four times the natural harvest. Who would have thought — "immeasurably more than all we could ask or imagine," from such inconsiderable beginnings. Not power, not might like we tend to think, or long to expect — not so much breakthrough power, but seed power — burying, dying, dormant power that in due season, yields.

And as Jesus tells it, there is an inevitability to this growth. I saw some astounding Google images that etched this forever in my mind. One of the hottest and driest places on earth is in California. Not surprisingly, the three thousand square miles in the rain shadow east of the Sierra Nevada Mountains is called Death Valley. It's not just hot; it's stinking hot. Furnace Creek holds the world's record for the hottest place on the planet: 134 F (56.7 C). In the summer of 2001, temperatures were over 100 degrees for one hundred fifty-four days. And it's spittin' dust dry. In the years 1929, 1953, and 1989, no rainfall fell — at all. But in the winter of 2005, six inches of rain soaked the Valley. That's four times its historic annual average. And come spring, Death Valley was ablaze with wild flowers. Seeds that had been dormant for decades, even centuries, burst forth and blanketed the desert floor. Pam Muick, executive director of the California Native Plant Society explained: "Death Valley isn't a wasteland. It will start looking empty when the flowers are gone, but there's life here at all times."[62]

There would be few of us who have never lived through a wasteland season of life — times when everything seemed barren, lifeless, even dead. That's why we need a graced understanding of the parable of the Sower. Regardless of how barren or fertile the soil, regardless of what comes against it, the Good News is that the seed does produce. Everything that is needed is there in the seed. Take the seed that is sown on the footpath and gobbled up by the birds. Which, in the interpretation, Jesus likened to Satan stealing away God's kingdom purpose. Birds recognise seed even if we don't, not unlike the demons recognising Jesus for who he was when many didn't. And birds who eat seed, and then fly away, eventually poop. In so doing, they cast seed further afield than the sower could do on his own. The Latin Church Fathers put it this way: *Ex malo bonum* — "Out of evil comes good." That's the Gospel. No matter the devil's schemes, the Word, like seed, still works on its own terms. There will come blessing, and redemption, and restoration. That's who our God is. That's what he does. That's why in Christ, all joy is ours. Not because things are the way they are, but because God is who he is, and the way grace works as it does. And notice this. In the other types of soil — the rocky ground, the weedy, or the fertile, the seed does what seed does. It germinates, generates, and brings forth life. It is not in any way dependent on circumstance or co-operation. The same seed, in the same good soil, produces different yields — some thirty, some sixty, some a hundred. Mystery.

Now, keep breathing, because I'm not saying that our response doesn't matter. *Au contraire.* The Gospel of the kingdom was and ever is proclaimed in a hostile world. There is the overtly demonic. There is the antagonism of the religious establishment, the careless indifference of the distracted, and the paralysis of the embittered. But nobody and nothing — not the devil, nor the world, nor our flesh — can keep us from the Love that will not let us go. If we're daft enough, we can try to wriggle free from his grip. We can despise his holding us. We can do everything in our power to refuse to be loved, and make a complete mess of things in doing so, but none of that changes the eternal fact that he loves us with a love that will not quit.

The seed that was eaten by the birds and then dumped is the

same seed that yielded a hundred fold. The seed scorched in the shallow soil and the seed choked out by worldly care all take place within the working of the kingdom, not prior to its coming or outside of it. Kingdom seed will bear fruit. That's the given. The Word's fruitfulness is not in question. What is in question is what difference the Word will make for us, to us, in us. Kingdom seed will bring forth life; will it bring forth life in us?

Hear the invitation of Jesus from John's Gospel:

> Dwell in me as I in you. No branch can bear fruit by itself, but only if it remains united with the vine; no more can you bear fruit, unless you remain united with me.... Anyone who dwells in me, as I dwell in him, bears much fruit; apart from me you can do nothing.[63]

Seventeen hundred years ago, St Augustine succinctly commented on this passage: *Aut vitus, aut ignis* — "fruit, or firewood." Think of the difference this way: the Apostle Paul said that "the works of the flesh are obvious: sexual immorality, impurity, depravity, idolatry, sorcery, hostilities, strife, jealousy, outbursts of anger, selfish rivalries, dissensions, factions, envying, murder, drunkenness, carousing, and similar things."[64] At end of day, that's a description of life when we try to meet our own needs, get our own way, and exercise control over our little worlds. Paul was contrasting things, and having described the works of the flesh, one would expect him to speak of the works of the Spirit. But he didn't balance his syntax, and for good reason. Theology trumps grammar. There's a supernatural, graced *more* at work in life, and so "the fruit of the Spirit is love, joy, peace, forbearance, kindness, goodness, faithfulness, gentleness, and self-control."[65]

At the end of the day, love, joy, peace, patience, kindness, goodness are that which make us truly, fully human. But gritting our teeth, and attempting to will love, or joy, or peace only produce spiritual haemorrhoids. It's not work; it's fruit. And how does an apple ripen? It sits in the sun. That being the case, one could conclude that Jesus bears most fruit in a life that interferes the least.

Notes

41. Romans 11.29
42. Ecclesiastes 9.10
43. Psalm 24.3-4, NIV.
44. Joshua 7
45. Mark 4.11-12
46. Revelation 21.1-2
47. 1Corinthians 1.31
48. Mark 4.12
49. John 3.17
50. Genesis 6 and 7
51. Genesis 9.12
52. Isaiah 53.4-5
53. Mark 4.11
54. Mark 4.13
55. See Mark 4.12
56. Mark 4.14
57. Mark 4.20; see Matthew 13.23
58. John 1.1-4
59. John 5.37-40
60. Mark 4.12
61. Matthew 13.57
62. Google: Death Valley 2005 – Images: Death Valley alive with wildflowers.
63. John 15.4-5
64. Galatians 5.19, NET. The Greek word is *erga*, from the root *ergon*, "works."
65. Galatians 5.22, NIV.

5
NEW WINESKINS

———•———

Years ago, I was privileged to preach in McAllen, Texas. The host church was a congregation of a thousand or so, and roughly a one-third split: white, black, Hispanic. For southwest Texas, that was quite remarkable. What made the week most remarkable was a group that came each evening. What set them apart was alternative hair colour. It was mostly green.

Each night, the leader, a guy with a stunning blue mohawk, would bring four or five green-hairs forward and say, "They're ready." (I guess that was the way it worked; when he said you were ready, you were ready.) I'd lead them to Jesus, and he'd pray with them as they gave their lives to the Lord.

The third night, the leadership team and I went out for something to eat after the meeting. After we'd ordered our food, the pastor's wife looked at me bug-eyed and gasped: "Those two girls I prayed for — they're *lesbians!*" I grinned and said, "Isn't it wonderful that they feel welcome enough to come," and before she could say anything I added something like, "You folks have been praying for revival. That won't just mean that backsliding Baptists find their way back home. If God grants you revival, church won't look the way church presently looks. Are you ok with that?"

Not everybody was ok with that. The alternative hair colour crowd came only to the evening meetings. And that spelt trouble in River City. Wallets were going missing from coats. Cars were being broken into, and radios stolen. I heard some of the congregational growling.

At the last morning meeting, I thanked the church for having me, and said how wonderful a privilege it was to have led forty or so green-hairs to the Lord. I said, "You've witnessed some amazing miracles over these last few days — among them, the miracle of sanctification. I know some of you have had your cars burgled, and radios stolen. That's very upsetting, but you can comfort yourself with this: the green-hairs are treating you as family, and have started walking in a new way of life. They're used to stealing the whole car." Then I said, "You have to decide which is of more value to you — lost souls, or lost radios."

———•———

Historically, an outpouring of God's Spirit redefines what it means to be church. Pneumatology — our understanding and experience of the Spirit — reshapes ecclesiology — our understanding and experience of the church. We can't receive 'more' and stay as we are. Our expectations, values, priorities — they all shift. There comes reformation, re-formation, unto greater health, greater fruitfulness, greater Kingdom fullness and blessing.

That necessarily means change. And that makes most people nervous. Jesus said, "No one puts new wine into old wineskins; if he does, the wine will burst the skins, and then wine and skins are both lost. New wine goes into fresh skins."[66] Jesus addressed those words to the Pharisees, the religious of the day, and he already had their knickers in a twist. But Jesus was unapologetic. He let them know that if it was up to him, things would not be *status quo*, 'the way it's always been done.' The reason? The Kingdom of heaven was upon them. Just as it is upon us.

What does that mean in terms of our wineskins, and what it means to be church, to 'do' church? First off, a fresh outpouring of the Spirit — new wine — means we have to attend to what has gotten old. What has lost its flexibility, its ability to stretch, to accommodate the expansion of the new? What's become, if not brittle, then stiff?

A church wineskin has become old when it's become religious, and then, stiffer still, a religious institution. We are religious when we feel compelled, or obliged, to keep the rules. Religion says, 'If you're good enough, God will be happy. Fail to measure up, and you endure his wrath.' Religion is first and foremost about ethical behaviour. Religion is a system of rights and wrongs, dos and don'ts. Religion determines who makes the grade, and who falls short. Religion determines who's in and who's out. Who's 'one of us,' and who's one of 'them.' Religion is fundamentally based on judgment.

Like a clumsy carpenter, the church has done a pretty good job of hitting the religious nail right on the thumb. It's telling that while many of us know John 3.16 by heart: "God so loved the world that he gave his only begotten Son…" not nearly so many have memorised the next verse: "It was not to judge the world that God sent his Son into the world, but that through him the world might be saved."[67]

Check this out: if you have one, is Matthew 7.1 underlined in your Bible? "Do not judge, and you will not be judged." How about Romans 5.8: "While we were still sinners, Christ died for us." Have you circled the "you" and the "us"? As soon as we name anybody who doesn't belong, we've lost the plot. We're facing a crisis of wineskins — an institutional rigidity. Something has become too stiff to extend grace — the same unconditional mercy and acceptance that we ourselves need.

I ran into this one hard, back in 1994. My first book, *Catch the Fire*, was published in October; in November, it featured on the cover of the *Canadian Baptist*, the monthly denominational magazine. The big, bold headline read: "Should Baptists 'Catch the Fire'?" Inside were fourteen pages of "No;" there was one sidebar of "Maybe."

A couple of months later, I was called before the credentials committee. For an hour and forty minutes, I answered their questions about what was being called the 'Toronto Blessing.' I answered questions about my itinerant ministry. And during that time, the chairman became more and more agitated. Veins stuck further and further out of his neck, and his jaws clenched more and more tightly. He finally exploded. "That's enough! You've completely failed to demonstrate any denominational loyalty whatsoever."

I looked at him, smiled and said, "Stan (not his real name), I've known you for fourteen years. Nothing's changed. I've never had any denominational loyalty. My devotion is not to an institution. I'm devoted to Christ and the work of his Kingdom." That was not the answer the credentials committee was looking for.

———•———

The church of Jesus Christ is first and foremost a community; an assembly of limping, scarred, and under-achieving human beings who are learning what it means to be drawn by love, and transformed by grace. At Pentecost, the church's 'birthday,' a new age was birthed. The Spirit of God was poured out on all flesh. Membership had only one requirement: you had to have a pulse.

Jump two thousand years; what does new wine, and new wine skins imply for us? We too, are limping, scarred and underachieving, learning to be drawn by love and transformed by grace. Whatever the way forward, one of the things it means for us is radical inclusivity, right at the very heart of our being: a wide, open welcome — for all. Just as we ourselves were received. Or hoped to be. How we yet need to be received.

Radical inclusivity, however, is only half the Gospel. We may not know the old hymn, but each and every one of us could come to God humming, *"Just as I am, thou wilt receive, Wilt welcome, pardon, cleanse, relieve; Because thy promise I believe, O Lamb of God, I come, I come."* We are welcomed just as we are; AND we are loved to become all that we yet shall be, in Christ. The church is to be a community of both radical inclusion, AND ongoing transformation. These two halves of the Gospel are what make us whole, and holy.

It would do us all good to pause here a moment and say, "Thank you, God, I'm not who I was, and bless you, Lord, I'm not whom I yet shall be." The new wine, and the new wineskin means: All in, and all being changed.

What holds the two in dynamic tension is repentance. *Metanoia* — once again, the word means, 'Change the way you think.' 'Change the way you see things.' There's good reason to do so, because God says, "My thoughts are not your thoughts, nor are your ways my ways.... As the heavens are high above the earth, so are my ways high above your ways, and my thoughts above your thoughts."[68] Repentance means we see that there is a world of difference between heaven and earth; the way God sees things, and the way we see things. Radical inclusivity and ongoing transformation are not a menu select, an either/or choice. The mandates are both/and. Forfeit — or compromise — either one, and it's like the old rhyme: 'An apple without the cheese is like a kiss without the squeeze.'

Notes

66. Mark 2.22
67. John 3.17
68. Isaiah 55.8

6
LOVE LOOKS LIKE LASAGNA

———•———

It's one thing to hear your barber say "Oops." It's another when your surgeon says it. Some things matter more than others.

———•———

One glorious autumn afternoon, a buddy and I were out golfing. As bright and sunny as the day was, it was evident that he was fussed, and I knew his disposition had nothing to do with his golf. His wife had recently gone for a tumble and was seriously injured. But that wasn't what he was stewing about. He's been an active part of his local church for years. His wife's pending surgery was posted on Facebook. What bothered my friend was the number of times his church family messaged him with assurances of their prayers, their condolences, and the concluding line: "Send your wife our love." Oops.

I'm in no way diminishing the power of prayer. But please — in a case like this, and you want to "send someone your love" know this: love looks like lasagna.

———•———

At seminary, one of the courses I took was called Practical Theology. The standing joke was that it implied that all our other courses were studies in IMpractical theology, and that's why the church is in the state she is. It's not a new problem.

Two thousand years ago the Apostle James faced the same disconnect:

> Suppose a fellow-Christian is in rags with not enough food for the day, and one of you says, 'Goodbye, keep warm, and have a good meal,' but does nothing to supply their bodily needs, what good is that? So with faith; if it does not lead to action, it is by itself a lifeless thing.[69]

I guess it's always been easy to rationalise. There's a crisis, a tragedy, or bad news of one sort or another, and we don't know what to say, so we mumble, 'I'll be praying for you.' And then we distance ourselves. 'It's none of my business.' 'That's a family matter.' 'We're not that close.'

Those are all really lame excuses. Faith that does not lead to action is a lifeless thing. But Jesus is the Lord and Giver of life. Yet full of 'faith,' the church so often misses the mark. Personally, it's a telling indictment that with a few very special exceptions, it has been my non-Christian golfing buddies who have come alongside me in my darkest hours. They're the ones who have been quick to say, "So sorry to hear your news. Can I take you out for a beer?" My cousin, not a church-goer, looked me straight in the eye and said, "You're blood. I'm going to get you through this." Were it not for his love, and the love of a few others who asked, "What do you need right now?" — there have been a number of times when I may not have made it.

Cleansing breath. There are many within the charismatic community of faith who pray regularly and faithfully for a greater prophetic gifting. They long to hear more of the voice of

God, and know more of the heart of God. Those are good and godly longings. But allow me a couple of test questions for those praying along these lines. When someone comes to mind, and you've thought, 'I should give them a call,' did you? How many of you have stood in front of someone, and you've thought, 'Boy, she looks sad.' What happened next?

Months ago, Kerry and I were checking into a hotel. Kerry looked at the receptionist and asked, "How are you today?" The woman had to blink back the tears as she said, "No one's ever asked me that before." Now, there was a queue behind us. Things didn't go any further than that. But at least there was something of connection.

If we don't pay attention to the subtle, gentle nudgings, the quiet stirrings of the Holy Spirit — to make a phone call, to write a note, to buy a beer, to make a lasagna — it's unlikely we'll being growing much in the prophetic. How could we? We're closing our ears to the voice of God. We're shutting our hearts to the heart of God. As the Apostle James said, "Faith divorced from action is dead."[70]

We're called to be a people who give *life*. Think of a time in your life when you were facing shipwreck. You know the desperate truth: in a crisis, you don't lose friends. You just find out who they really are. In an earlier chapter, I told of the distress I suffered when my fiancé announced that she was in love with someone else. She dropped this bombshell just as I was about to start writing exams. For over a week, my buddy Al sat with me all day long, reading motorcycle magazines while I tried to study. When I'd start to freak out, he'd listen for a while, and then he'd say, "Hit the books for another hour, then we'll go for a ride."

Kindness, more than any other thing, heals the cancer of

loneliness. In our time of need, what makes the difference are simple, practical kindnesses. Kindness isn't tricky. It isn't sophisticated. It doesn't require a great deal of wisdom, or even discernment. And that's Good News, because it means that it's quite hard to get kindness wrong. Who doesn't like lasagna?

With the following, I'm going to date myself. If you can, you may remember a song from the eighties by a band called Foreigner. Lou Gramm put words to the soul's longing as he crooned, "I want know what love is; I want you to show me…"

We of all people ought to have the answer. Love looks like lasagna.

Notes
69. James 2.15-17
70. James 2.26

7
WHO'S TELLING YOU WHAT?

—·—

In 1973, I memorised Romans 8 — the entire chapter. It was the longest passage of Scripture I have ever committed to memory, and I've meditated on that single chapter more than any other. The thing is, in reading Romans, verse by verse, even chapter by chapter, I find it very easy to lose the proverbial forest for the trees.

It helps to keep something of context in mind. What we call the Book of Romans is a letter that Paul wrote to a church in Rome. They were a mixed congregation, and a divided one. A congregation that could potentially split. That rupture would not only have been horrendous for the church family in Rome; if they split there would have been serious repercussions for the young church throughout the Empire, many of which were also mixed congregations.

In his letter Paul addressed two audiences — Jew and Gentile — two people groups that were radically different. The Jewish believers had a strict, religious and exclusive life based on the Torah, the Jewish Scriptures. The Gentile believers were a far more eclectic mix of cultural, philosophical, and pagan influences. So there were in this one church, People of the Law, and the Law-less.

Two things were at stake. First, was the Gospel bigger than

these very big differences? And second, could the young church hold these two polarised groups together? Paul wanted this young church to understand that regardless of their background and their orientation, they were one Body in Christ, under his Lordship. In him, they had a new allegiance and a new identity. More, they had a new self-understanding. One that was greater than wherever they came from, and whatever they'd grown up with; one that was greater than their traditions, their cultures, and their personal histories.

That's why he wrote the letter — but he had his work cut out for himself. And so do we, because it is not easy going. The Apostle went to great lengths to get the Jewish believers, the religious, to understand that God only justifies sinners. Paul rocked their kosher world with this declaration: "No human being can be justified in the sight of God by keeping the law."[71] Now remember, he wrote this to a people who had devoted themselves to religious performance; a people who laboured to measure up, who walked a very narrow path. Their whole identity was based on keeping all the rules and regulations.

And Paul took a wrecking ball to the whole construct. Because in Christ, there is nothing to be earned, nothing that is deserved, and absolutely nothing of merit. It's all and only mercy, and the power of God's grace.

A couple of chapters later, he laid the foundational bedrock of the Gospel: "God demonstrates (present tense) his own love for us in this: While we were still sinners, Christ died for us."[72] Grammatically, Paul knew that his subjects and predicates should agree. He knew that he should have written in the past tense: 'God demonstratED his love....' The past tense would agree with the past tense event of Jesus' death two thousand years ago. But God is still demonstrating his love for us, in the midst of our current sin. Christ's death two thousand years ago covers our present failures. Christ died for us while we are still a proper mess.

If that weren't scandal enough, Paul took things further. Over the next two chapters, he was at pains to show that it's not just that we don't have to earn God's approval and acceptance; Paul made it clear that we can't. If it were possible for us to 'get our act together,' some of us over-achievers would have done so by now. But we haven't, because we can't. (As I write this, it's the 26th of January. One month into things, how were you doing with your New Year's resolutions? I know, I know — it was a hard month.) I agree with the Apostle Paul. The things I want to do, I often don't end up doing. And there are times I do things... that I don't want to do. And when I do manage to do the things I want to do, they often don't end up quite the way I thought they would. My best efforts amount to wiggling in quicksand. There's no bottom. Without help, I'll never be able to get myself out.[73]

And that brings us to Romans, chapter 8. "Therefore..." That's Paul's conclusion, the "So what?" to all that he laid out in the previous seven chapters: "Therefore, there is now no condemnation for those who are in Christ Jesus." A moment's reflection: We're all subject to the little voices, the whispering voices. (Right now, some of you are thinking, 'I don't hear little voices'....) If, in your heart of hearts, you hear a little voice that condemns, you are listening to a word that God is not speaking. *"What good are you?" "You expect God to forgive that, again???" "You are such a loser."* That rubbish is coming from another source. In Revelation 12.10, Satan is called 'the Accuser,' and ultimately you can lay all condemnation at his feet, because condemnation is never from the heart of God.

My job is to move this truth eighteen inches, because we need to know this truth not just with our heads, but in our hearts. Otherwise we won't know the fullness of freedom that is ours in Christ.

Paul asked, "Who will bring a charge against those whom God has chosen?"[74] He answered: "It is God who acquits." Other translations say, "it is God who justifies." Others, "God finds no fault." Eugene Peterson in *The Message* paraphrases, "Who would dare even to point a finger?" The Apostle Paul asked again, "Who then is the one who condemns?" The answer resounds: "Christ Jesus who died — more than that, who was raised to life — is at the right hand of God and is also interceding for us."[75] There's the question, as stark and as un-adorned as it can be asked — Who is he that condemns?

At first blush it doesn't look like it was answered as straightforwardly as it was asked. But Paul already answered the question, just a few verses earlier. Who is he that condemns? "There is now no condemnation for those who are in Christ Jesus."[76] And a couple of verses later, he explained why: God sent his own Son "in the likeness of sinful man to be a sin offering. And so he condemned sin…."[77]

We could easily end up in deep weeds here, so let me offer this. Most of us were raised on 'fair.' We were rewarded when we were good, and punished when we were bad. "Be a good boy, and you can have a cookie." "Do that again, and it's straight to your room!" At school: gold stars, or the head teacher's office. Again. At work: promotions, or pink slips.[78] Religion: any one you want to pick — the righteous are rewarded; the wicked are punished, if not in this life, then in a hot and miserable afterlife.

Most of us have difficulty moving beyond 'fair,' and it shows in all sorts of ways. If you've been in church for a while, you'll remember church banners. Thirty years ago, one of the popular ones had all the different names of Jesus on it. *Mighty God; Prince of Peace; Emmanuel; Lamb of God; Alpha and Omega; Resurrection and the Life.* One name never made it on any banner I ever saw. *Scandal.* It's a telling omission. An understandable one, because it's so unsettling. Paul said, "We preach Christ crucified: a stumbling block to Jews and foolishness to Gentiles." Scandal and folly, because what God has done for us in Christ is not fair.

Santa is fair. When Santa comes to town, he's 'made up his list, he's checked it through twice; he's figured out who's been naughty or nice.' When Jesus comes to town, that's not the song he's singing.

See if this helps. Almost five hundred years ago the theological architect of the Protestant Reformation, John Calvin, wrote his life's work, *Institutes of the Christian Religion.* He called the third part of the *Institutes* "The Way in Which We Receive the Grace of Christ: What Benefits Come to Us from It, and What Effects Follow." In the second chapter, Calvin wrote about "the treasures of grace that are opened to us."[79] He offered the following by way of illustration. (I've embellished it just a bit.) Let's pretend for a moment that I am stupidly wealthy. Pretend that I have more money than I know what to do with. And let's say I like to do fun things with it, 'cause I'm a fun kind of guy.

One night, just for a lark, I sneak through your side gate and bury a box full of gold bars worth one million pounds — south-side alleyway, under your wheely bin. I phone you the next morning. After I introduce myself I tell you what I've done. "Yes I'm serious. A million pounds worth of gold, south-side alleyway." Then I say, "I don't mean to freak you out, but I happen to know there's enough there to pay off all of your debts, and that there's lots left over. Enough for you to thoroughly enjoy yourself for the rest of your life."

I assure you that I have no intention of ever taking the money back. It's yours, forever. There are no strings attached. You owe me absolutely nothing. I'm just stupidly wealthy, and I like flipping people out, and it's your lucky day. "Ta-rah."

You hang up the phone, and you have a choice. You could decide that I am not a loon. You could trust me. You realise that all that gold doesn't do you any good just sitting there underneath your wheely bin, so you go and get a shovel, head for the south-side alleyway, roll the bin out of the way, and make my gift yours. In technical theological terms, you appropriate my gift.

See, you have to make it yours in order to use it. But you are also perfectly free to conclude that I am indeed a lunatic, and that my offer is too good to be true. You could keep on living hand to mouth, pay-packet to pay-packet, flat broke at the end of every month. The thing is, none of that changes the fact that there's a million pounds worth of gold buried at the side of your house.

You could, one day, just out of curiosity, wonder about my good news. You could, just on the off chance, decide to scratch around in the dirt for a couple of minutes, and then run back indoors and book a fantastic holiday in the south of Spain.

See, the fortune is yours. It's buried at the side of your house. Technically, you have legal title to it. But you're no richer unless you dig it up and start spending it. And just in case you haven't been paying attention — you've done absolutely nothing to deserve the gift. In fact, what you have or have not done has absolutely nothing to do with anything here. Whether or not you've been 'naughty or nice' doesn't play here. I'm just stupidly wealthy, and I get a kick out of sharing my wealth. I happened to pick you to share it with.

Your trust, or your faith in me and what I've done for you —

believing that I actually did such a crazy thing — it has absolutely no bearing on the fact that I've buried the gold in your alleyway. The gold is there, whether or not you believe me. Your faith plays absolutely no part in causing me to give you the gift. I've already given it you — before you knew it was there. *Your faith simply enables you to enjoy my gift.*

I know it's a struggle. We want to know how all this works. Here's the best way I know of to explain the complexities of the atoning sacrifice of Christ: think of the Terms and Conditions for Microsoft Office. If you have carefully studied the twenty-four pages of legalese may I suggest it may be time for you to get a hobby. I've never read my way through the first paragraph. There's more there than mere mortals can even begin to comprehend. I trust that the thing is going to work, which was a huge leap of faith before I went Mac. I just click 'AGREE' and get on with it.

Time and again, in scripture after scripture, God has said that as far as he is concerned the condemnation issues are sorted. Jesus has done all that needs doing, and has dealt with all that needs dealing with. His life trumps death. The power of his grace is greater than the power of sin. His love reverses the curse. In him, ours are the blessings of heaven. Our debts are more than paid for; there's lots left over; enough for us to thoroughly enjoy ourselves for the rest of our lives. AGREED?

Without diminishing your euphoria in any way, a quick word about conviction. The Holy Spirit does convict us of sin. That's one of his jobs. He brings merciful revelation that we're out of line. He warns us that if we continue on the course we're heading, we'll forfeit our freedom and peace. He calls us out of darkness, into the light. For instance, for those of you who are reading through this book slowly, you might recall the first chapter; as you've gone about your business, how many times have you heard quiet little whisperings, "Commit to kindness"?

If we come into agreement with the Holy Spirit, his stirrings and promptings call forth conviction, and they initiate repentance — they change the way we see things. That change of mind then empowers redemption, the making of all things new, which in turn yields sanctification, the wholeness and holiness that God purposes. Conversely, if we come into agreement with the Accuser, condemnation breeds self-loathing, it feeds fear, and it ends in further oppression. So we have a choice. If we are to know the freedom and the fullness that Jesus purposes for us, we need to be ever-attentive to conviction, and deaf to condemnation. We need to be able to discern the difference between conviction and condemnation — in a heartbeat.

So many in the church are way too hard on themselves. Let me put it differently; many find fault with themselves in ways that God does not. If that's you, hear this by way of a reminder: God is God; you're not. If he does not find fault with you — "there is now no condemnation in Christ" — why do you keep beating up on yourself?

This is still a big deal for all manner of us, so let me go round the loop one more lap. I moved to England November 1st, 2013. It then took considerable time and effort to establish my life in Britain. I had to apply for citizenship, and then a passport, and then National Health Insurance; I had to sort banking, car insurance, and my driver's license.

I've been driving since I was sixteen years old. Over the years, I've had two speeding tickets, the last one back in 1987. I've never had an accident. My insurance rates reflected a 'perfect' driving record.

I've had a Visa card since I was twenty-two. I rarely use cash. I use my credit card whenever I can, because at month's end Visa is kind enough to give me a detailed record of my spending. But let the record show: in thirty-seven years, I have never paid a penny of interest. I have a 'perfect' credit rating.

Do you know what the British insurance companies and the banks thought of all of that? With one voice, they made it very clear: "We're very sorry Sir, but we can't take your history into account. None of it applies here."

Take all of that, and flip it into grace. The Trinity call a special meeting. They review my *im*perfect credit history, my debt, my multiple infractions and 'accidents,' and with one voice, they say exactly the same thing — with a graced addition: "We're very sorry Sir, but we can't take your history into account. None of it applies here. Here, 'there is now no condemnation for those who are in Christ Jesus.'"

Dear reader, I bless you with open ears. May you attentively hear the loving call of the Spirit — unto life. I bless you with a yielded spirit — that you have ears to hear his convicting grace. And I bless you with glorious, graced deafness.

I bet I'm the first author to ever bless you with deafness, but may you be stone deaf to the condemning, fault-finding accusations that steal your joy, and rob your peace, and torment you soul.

Notes
71. Romans 3.20
72. Romans 5.8, NIV.
73. See Romans 7.21-25
74. Romans 8.33
75. Romans 8.34, NIV.

76. Romans 8.1, NIV.

77. Romans 8.3, NIV.

78. A pink slip is slang for a termination notice. In the UK, its equivalent would be a P45.

79. John Calvin, *Institutes of the Christian Religion*, trans FL Battles, Philadelphia, Westminster Press, 1960, Bk III, Ch II.6, p.548.

8
NERF GOSPEL

I recently read a book titled *The Mystery of Christ*.[80] In it there was an illustration I've been thinking about ever since. A Nerf ball was used to talk about life. For those unfamiliar with a Nerf ball, it's a soft squishy ball the size of a softball, designed to be played with indoors. While a Nerf ball won't damage a wall on impact, it can knock lamps to the floor, and most of the time, they smash. I've experimented.

In the illustration, a Nerf ball — not nerd, as spell-check keeps trying to insist — is like my life, your life, every life. In each of our lives, there is a certain softness, a receptivity. I know it's not a word, but an imprint-ability.

Every one of us has a dent or two. Ok, more. Every one of us has been scuffed and scarred, mashed and marred. Some we've done to ourselves, some has been done to us. For instance, our parents and our care-givers leave imprints on our lives, and not all of those imprints are good ones. Statistically, ninety-four per cent of us are from dysfunctional homes. (The other six per cent are in denial.) Even those who feel they were raised in happy, healthy homes nevertheless have woundings and scars from their upbringing.

One of my imprints happened when I was six, and while it isn't a particularly big or deep dent, it is nonetheless a significant one. I used my allowance to buy my mother several packs of flower seeds. I wrapped them as neatly as a clumsy six-year old could, and proudly presented them to her on Mother's Day. It was evident that she was not impressed with my offering. My father came to my defence and said, "It's not the gift but the thought that counts." To which my mother responded, "Like hell it is."

It wasn't until my adult years that I learned of the mistreatment my mother had suffered as a child. It was years later still that I learned of some of the long-standing problems my mom and dad endured as a couple. On that seed-packet Mother's Day, in hindsight, there are pretty good odds that mom was finding fault more with my father than she was with me, but at the time, I took it personally. That denting imprint played a part in fuelling the 'never good enough,' 'never get it right' complex, and it was decades before I was mature enough to forgive her.

Forgive, because there are no perfect parents. The love we long for, the love we need — the perfect love, the perfect nurture, the perfect care, no one of us received from our parents. There's a rather strange verse in Matthew's Gospel that suddenly makes sense in this context. Jesus said, "Do not call any man on earth 'father,' for you have one Father, and he is in heaven."[81] The perfect love we long for we only receive from our Heavenly Father. And there will be distortion so long as we expect perfect love from our parents. They can't give it to us; only our Heavenly Father can.

But it's not just our family of origin that leaves imprints. In junior high school, I was beat up nearly every day — for being a nerd. (Yes, spell-check, nerd.) I hated recess, and dreaded lunchtime. The beatings didn't stop until the day I beat up my best friend Rusty. Then I was no longer the last and the least of the under-dogs.

The fat lips, and the bruises, and the knots on my head healed over time; the dents to my self-image, and the scars on my self-understanding took years to sort. In the mean time, along came love. Love that sadly wasn't always reciprocated, and didn't always last. That meant that there were the dumpers, and the dumpees. By and large I was the one that got dumped, and that left imprints. And so it goes, for each and every one of us. We all have imprint stories of pain, grief, and wounding. All in, it's quite remarkable that any one of us function as well as we do.

That's the sad, sorry news. Now the Good News in Jesus Christ. He did not come to judge, but to save. God didn't look at my life, and say "You are a *right* mess, aren't you?" No. He knew precisely what was wrong with me, and yet purposes to restore all things. This has always been his way. Seventeen hundred years ago, one of the Church Fathers, Athanasius, said: "Christ became what we are, that we might become as he is." Think of the deliverance of the most demonised man in the Bible. He was so tormented his demons had demons. He lived in a cemetery; he was only at 'home' when surrounded by death. He was a serial self-harmer, and he was out of his mind. He believed his name was Legion. That's a semi-technical nickname. A legion was a unit of six thousand men in the Roman army. In Mark's account, all those demons were cast into a large herd of swine, "about two thousand in number."[82] Legion's demons — six thousand of them, into a herd of two thousand pigs — they charged over a cliff and drowned in the lake.

Do the maths: three demons per pig were enough to drive them crazy to destruction. Which is one more way of saying that this guy Legion was seriously tormented. But only until he met Jesus, because the peace within Jesus was so much greater than the torment within Legion. His peace is so much greater than our torments.

The story ends with Ex-legion "clothed, sitting at feet of Jesus, in his right mind." He was at peace with himself. He was restored. Nearly five hundred years ago the great Reformer, John Calvin, called this restorative work "The Wondrous Exchange." He described it like this:

> Out of his boundless goodness, becoming Son of Man with us, Jesus has made us sons of God with him; that, by his descent to earth, he has prepared an ascent to Heaven for us; that, by taking on our mortality, he has conferred his immortality upon us; that, accepting our weakness, he has strengthened us with his power; that, receiving our poverty unto himself, he has transferred his wealth to us; that, taking the weight of our iniquity upon himself, he has clothed us with his righteousness.[83]

This Wondrous Exchange is the purpose for Christ's coming. Jesus himself said, "The Son of Man has come to seek and to save what is lost."[84] *Sozo*, the Greek root word translated "to save," is a big, fluid word meaning "to save, to heal, to make whole, to restore." What God purposes in Jesus is cosmic redemption, the redemption and restoration of all of creation, all that's been mashed and marred by sin. The million-dollar question, is how?

In my late teens, I had a buddy named Doug. In his last year of high school, he earned a squash scholarship from an Ivy League University. In preparation, he played so much squash that he separated his shoulder. When the Ivy Leaguers found that out, they didn't want him.

Doug and I went to a local university together, and he taught me how to play squash. The first year, we'd step into the court with our racquets, a ball, and two pieces of butcher's twine — one for him, one for me. He'd get me to tie his right elbow tight to his side so he couldn't use that arm at all. I'm left handed, and I'd played some tennis. He'd tie a loop around my left elbow, and a loop around my waist, and give me a mere four inches of slack. That way, instead of a big, armsy tennis swing, I was forced to learn to use my wrist and flick the racket. It also meant that he didn't get whacked so often as I flailed about.

All the while, Doug was retraining, re-scripting, and unlearning the dominance of his right hand. Awkwardly at first, shot after shot, he was taking all of his squash knowledge and flipping it, from right to left. He did such a good job that in three years he became Number Three seed on the Varsity squash team — playing left handed.

Neuroscientists could use Doug as a poster child for what they call brain plasticity, because the ways in which a brain responds, reacts, and processes are malleable. We are not hardwired with unchangeable circuitry. We can re-format the ways in which we do things, and the ways in which we process. Like re-training hand dominance, right, to left.

———•———

Back to life as a Nerf ball. There are two grips on the ball, on my life. There's mine, and all that I'm trying to do to manage the dents, and imprints, the scuffs and the scars of life. And there is also the Lord's hand. Jesus is holding my life, as he holds "all things together."[85]

In his grip, my life is no longer a mess. There is a graced resilience. A bounce-back, if you will, to what I was made and meant to be, before all the denting and imprinting, the scuffing and the scarring. In his grip, there is restoration and redemption. There is re-creation, because love is stronger than abuse.

Now, the two grips — left and right hand, mine and Jesus' — are going on at that same time. But I won't know the power of his until I let go of mine. My dominant hand had the firmest grip on things for the first twenty years of my life. Since then, I have been learning to let his hand be the dominant one. I still have some Bozo moments when I think I can do a better job sorting things than Jesus can, but most of the time, I know his grip of grace.

A few of you are almost screaming, "How?"

The Good News is that there's absolutely nothing for you to do, nothing you can or need to do, except — "Repent, and believe the Gospel." Repentance — that Greek word *metanoia* again — is two words pasted together: *meta + nous* — 'turn', and 'mind'. Repentance means 'change the way you think'. Re-script. Re-format. Process things differently.

The dents and the distortion — that's what's been done to you. The restoration — the 'bounce-back' is what has been done *for* you. In Jesus, "our release is secured." The Apostle Paul assured us of that repeatedly.[86] That's the Good News. We're not on our own in this. It's not just an act-of-the-will decision, 'transformation through clenched teeth.'

Jesus said: "A thief comes only to steal, kill and destroy; I have come that you might have life, and have it in all its fullness."[87] Life in its abundance. Each of us have had something of our lives stolen; we can each trace a measure of destruction over our histories; we each suffer something of a sickness unto death. That's the human condition — without Jesus. But just as he restored the man with the withered arm, so Jesus purposes to restore that which is atrophied in us. To restore what's been fractured, scarred, broken, wounded, abused, rejected, dishonoured. That's the Gospel: "The kingdom of God is upon you. Repent, and believe the Good News."[88]

Right now, the Holy Spirit is brooding over us, covering us... saving us, healing us, restoring us. Now might be a very good time to say, 'Thank you Jesus, that you hold my life in the grip of your grace. Thank you that you *are* Redeemer. Restorer. Healer. Thank you that your love covers my life. My dents. The scars. The wounds. Thank you that the power of your love is greater than the abuse that I've suffered. Thank you that in your grace, all things are made new, my life included. Amen.'

———•———

I've been around enough to know that there are some dear folks who don't feel like their life has been dented... but rather, squished. There are some who are saying, *"I can't..."* (Fill in your own blank.) *"I can't"* is, one way or another, a death sentence. *"I can't"* kills hope, it kills peace, it kills freedom. *"I can't"* kills both your present and your future in God. But Jesus has overcome death. He has taken captivity captive. He is restoring all things. For sake of argument, let's say that indeed, you can't. He can.

Decades ago, I read somewhere that every act of faith requires a renunciation. For instance, Jesus said to Simon and Andrew, "'Come, follow Me,' and at once, they left their nets and followed Him."[89] Faith ... and renunciation. In order for there to be a turning to, there has to be a turning from.

Some of you have realised as never before that in order to know the Lord's redeeming, restoring work of grace, you have to let go. I know, you have a fear of losing control. You have a fear of being out of control. You've done a good job being in control. On your own, you've needed to, in order to survive. The thing is, we're not meant just to survive. And you're not on your own.

Jesus purposes that we prosper. He purposes our well-being. He purposes blessing and abundance.

When it comes to control, he does a brilliant job.

Notes

80. Robert Capon, *The Mystery of Christ*, Eerdmans, Grand Rapids Michigan, 1993, p.128.
81. Matthew 23.9
82. Mark 5.13, NIV.
83. *Institutes of the Christian Religion*, Book IV, Chapter XVII.2, trans. F.L. Battles, Philadelphia: Westminster Press, 1960, p.1362.
84. Luke 19.10
85. Colossians 1.17, NIV.
86. Ephesians 1.7 and Colossians 1.14
87. John 10.10
88. Mark 1.15 NIV.
89. See Mark 1.17-18

9

UNGOOGLING EARTH — AND OUR HEARTS

I amuse easily, so I've probably spent more time fooling around with the Google Earth app than I should have. If you haven't used it, download it and have a bit of fun. Google Earth starts up with a picture of the globe, and then it starts zooming in, and all on its own, the world turns, first the continent, then the country, then the county, then the community, and there — not just the neighbourhood — but our actual street address. It's amazing! I think that is so cool!

Spiritually, there is something in us that does exactly the same thing. Only it's not so amazing. Not so cool. It's a real problem. Google Earth has as a built-in default that uses the present GPS co-ordinates, and so when we click on it, our current location — where we are — becomes the focal point. Everything zooms in on that, from God's big wide world, to wherever it is we find ourselves.

We have a built-in default that does the same. We go from God's big wide world, to where we are — we are ever the focal point, the centre of our own little universe. Everything zooms in on us. And it's not just a default; it's a defect.

Now, don't panic, but we're going to rehearse a teeny weeny bit of philosophy. Just for a few minutes, we're going to consider what's called Cartesian egocentricity. Almost four hundred years ago there was a French philosopher and mathematician named Rene Descartes. He was both brilliant and arrogant. Both brilliance and arrogance are pretty much required if you're going to be a great philosopher. Brilliance isn't a surprise, but arrogance?

Descartes was so sure of himself that he challenged the way traditional religion and philosophy understood life, the universe and just about everything. In an opening section to one of his books, he declared: "I will write as if no one had written on these matters before."

Descartes is most famously known for his statement, *Cogito ergo sum*, "I think, therefore I am." And that brings us back to where we started, because with that statement, Descartes went from God's big wide world, and he — Descartes — became the centre of the universe, just like Google Earth. Descartes' zoom in focal point was on the "I": "I think... I am..."

Descartes wasn't alone. *Cogito ergo sum* defines our default to self-preoccupation. We're always thinking about ourselves. Right now, I'm quite hot. I'm thirsty. I'm getting a little bit hungry. Maybe you're thinking, "I'm getting really bored." Patience: what we think defines reality for us. It's the way it is. If I'm upset, it's because I perceive my life circumstances to be upsetting. If I'm anxious, it's because I perceive my circumstances to be unsettled and uncertain.

Those of you who are bored — it's because you perceive this meditation to be boring. There are some — not many, I concede — but some, who think this is great stuff. And you're both reading the same text! It's your perception that's different, not the reflection.

There isn't a person here who hasn't, at some point or another, thought, 'My life sucks.' Remember — what we think defines reality for us. It's the way it is. If we think our lives suck, it's because we perceive our life circumstances to be sucky. We've zoomed in on our problems, be it our debt, or our insane teenagers. Our ill-health. Our loveless marriage. Our selfish boyfriend. Our jealous girlfriend. We 'Google Earth' our lives, and our problems become our current location, and the centre of our very little universe.

———•———

I started thinking about all of this while I was meditating on the passage where the rich young ruler came to Jesus and asked, "Teacher, what good must I do to gain eternal life?" Jesus answered, "'Good'? Why do you ask me about that? One alone is good."[90] The Lord's answer seemed strange to me. Of all people, Jesus could honestly say that he was good — and that's what got me thinking — Jesus never suffered from Cartesian egocentricity. He never considered himself the centre of the universe. Rather, he lived a re-calibrated life.

In John's Gospel for instance, Jesus was on his way to Jerusalem, knowing he would soon be laying down his life. He said to his disciples, "Now my soul is in turmoil, and what am I to say? 'Father, save me from this hour'? No, it was for this very reason that I came to this hour. Father, glorify your name."[91]

Most of us aren't there. And again, our Cartesian egocentricity — our self-preoccupation — isn't just a default; it's a defect that costs us. Try this: when things get tough, really tough, tough for a really long time, do those troubling circumstances change your understanding of the goodness of God, or does the unchanging goodness of God change your understanding of those same circumstances?

"One alone is good." That's God's unchanging character: "The Lord is gracious and compassionate, long-suffering and ever faithful. The Lord is good to all; his compassion rests upon all his creatures."[92] "Every good and perfect gift is from above, coming down from the Father of the heavenly lights, who does not change…"[93]

When things get tough for Kerry and me, we comfort and encourage each other with these words: "This is what God's love looks like for us right now."

————•————

A couple of pages ago, I said that Descartes was both brilliant and arrogant. Arrogance is defined as "an exaggerated sense of one's own importance." It comes from the root word, *arrogate*, "to claim for oneself." Anxiety is a function of arrogance. Answer this question: What are you currently anxious about? After you sigh and say, "Well…", what's the next word? "I…" Anyone have something different? How about "My…"

When we're anxious, we may have an exaggerated sense that our life circumstances should be different than they are. If so, we want to claim for ourselves something that we presently don't have.

————•————

The Sermon on the Mount is about Kingdom living, and Kingdom living is grounded in Kingdom relationship. In the middle of the sermon, Jesus grounded his teaching on prayer with these words: "Your Father knows what your needs are before you ask him."[94] Jesus then asked the bare-bones question, "Why be anxious?"[95] A couple of verses earlier, he asked why we are anxious about food and drink and clothes.[96] Food, drink, clothes, unlimited broadband access — these are life's basics, life's essentials. We can't live without them.

Let the question stand in all its simplicity — Why be anxious? Jesus named the reason for our anxiety: "How little faith you have."[97] And then He ungoogled things: "Your heavenly Father knows your needs."[98] In other words, if we had more faith, we would trust our heavenly Father's goodness.

Let me ask my earlier questions again: Do troubling circumstances change your understanding of the goodness of God, or does the unchanging goodness of God change your understanding of those same circumstances? "Why be anxious? How little faith you have. Your heavenly Father knows your needs."

Let's connect a few more dots. Our heavenly Father doesn't just know our needs. He "is able to make all grace abound to [us], so that in all things at all times, having all that [we] need, [we] may abound in every good work."[99]

————·————

Back to Google Earth and everything zooming in on our current location. When I become self-preoccupied, when I zoom in on my little life, it's like I go in too closely. Things get fuzzy. They lose their definition. I lose all sense of perspective.

Back in March, Kerry and I were hiking in the Brecon Beacons, Wales. On the top of Black Mountain, the fog descended. I knew where I was... but I'd lost the horizon. The same thing happens spiritually. In my anxiety, my worry, my disappointment, the fog descends and I can't see anything beyond that. I lose the sense of where I'm going.

Every anxious thought is like fog that obscures our vision of the goodness of God. Every fearful thought fogs our understanding of the unfailing love of God. Every doubtful thought fogs our experience of the faithfulness of God.

Now, the fog of worry, fear, and doubt descend, not because we don't have enough faith. We do. We just have misplaced faith. We have faith in our troubling circumstances, how things appear to us, and catastrophically, how they'll always be that way. We do not have faith in the redeeming, restorative, unfailing goodness of

God, at work in those very circumstances.

It's one of the reasons we worship. More than anything else, worship clears the fog. As we worship, we recalibrate our perceptions, our realities. Worship re-calibrates how we see our lives, and our circumstances. We recover our horizons, and the sense of where we're heading.

This is how King David did it: "Listen, Lord, and give me an answer, for I am oppressed and poor... Show me your favour... for to you, Lord, I lift up my heart." (There — right there — is the re-calibration — "to you, Lord, I lift up my heart" — up, beyond whatever it is we're facing, whatever it is we're having to deal with — whatever it is that has our hearts all tangled.) "Lord, you are kind and forgiving, full of love towards all who cry to you... You are great, and your works are wonderful; you alone are God... Your love towards me is great... for you, Lord, are God, compassionate and gracious, long-suffering, ever faithful and true...."[100]

As we declare the goodness of God, the unfailing love of God, the faithfulness of God, our worship enables us to zoom out, because we have magnified the Lord. We've made him bigger than our worries, and our fears, and our doubts.

This is what it means for our spirits to rule over our souls. Our souls are all in a tangle... but our spirits re-calibrate how we see things, and how we respond to things. It's one of the big tests of spiritual maturity. When the pressure increases, and it feels like we're at breaking point, do we spit the dummy, pull a strop, have a full-blown freak out — or — in the midst of it all, do we pray as Jesus did: "Father, glorify your name."

————•————

The title of this meditation is "Ungoogling Earth — and our hearts." Now it's time for the big question: *how* do we ungoogle our hearts? How do we shift the self-preoccupation that has us focusing on our own little worlds?

What works for me is to confess my anxious thoughts, my fears, my doubts, rather than to stew in them. Something along these lines: "Father, oh Father, I've got myself lost, again. I've zoomed in, and all I see is... well.... not very much at all. I've got myself all wound up again, all tangled up again. Please forgive me."

Then, I give thanks.

"Thank you, Father, that your love never fails. Jesus, thank you that right now, you are holding my all together. Thank you, Lord, that you purpose immeasurably more than all I can see or understand."

I back up and pray from the earlier part of Paul's great apostolic prayer in Ephesians 3.16, that "out of the treasures of his glory he would grant inner strength and power in my innermost being." Strength for what? To know the "breadth and length and height and depth of Christ's love, and to know it though it's beyond knowledge." To know the boundless, limitless, incomprehensible love of Christ — especially when I haven't a clue what the hang is going on.

And then I start singing, and keep singing until the fog clears.

Notes
90. Matthew 19.16-17
91. John 12.27
92. Psalm 145.8
93. James 1.17, NIV.
94. Matthew 6.8
95. Matthew 6.28
96. Matthew 6.25
97. Matthew 6.30
98. See Matthew 6.32
99. See 2 Corinthians 9.8-9, NIV, 1984.
100. Psalm 86.1, 3-5, 10, 13, 15

10
THERE IS A COMFORT

Some time ago I was in a boutique bakery-coffee shop, and posted on the front door was a sign that made me howl. It read: *"Unattended children will be given a complimentary espresso and a free kitten."* It's a very declarative statement, but one which requires some interpretation.

I subsequently thought that it's a very good way to understand the prophetic: declarative, but requiring some interpretation. The word of the Lord is rarely so unadorned as to say the coffee shop equivalent of "Parents, mind your children."

About the same time I was reading in the Book of Acts, and that bakery sign served as helpful commentary on a rather strange passage of Scripture. Prior to heading off on a missions trip, the Apostle Paul, raised Jewish, had his companion Timothy, raised Gentile, undergo circumcision.[101] Just so there's no misunderstanding, circumcision is a distinctively Jewish practice. The thing is, this is the same Paul who wrote that great declaration in his letter to the Galatians:

It is for freedom that Christ has set us free. Stand firm therefore, and refuse to submit again to the yoke of slavery. Mark my words... if you get yourself circumcised Christ will benefit you no more.... Every man who accepts circumcision is under obligation to keep the entire law.[102]

My guess is that when Timothy read that, he wanted a word or two with Paul.

——•——

The second part of the missions story in Acts 16 require no less interpretation. The Holy Spirit prevented Paul and Timothy from preaching in Asia.[103] Now, that's a little odd if you think of the Great Commission to go "into all the world."[104] Last time I looked, that included Asia.

Without any explanation or clarification, the Apostles then received a vision that redirected them to Macedonia, and convinced them that God was calling them to take the Good News there. They headed to Philippi, a major city in Macedonia, preached a bit, casted out a demon of bother, and promptly got arrested. After a severe beating, they were thrown into prison.[105] That had to leave them thinking, "*That* went well…."

I'm certainly left wondering: as they were having the daylights thrashed out of them, might they not have been quite so convinced this was God's call on their lives? And it then causes me to ponder; for all the prophetic words that have been spoken over my life, everything isn't quite unfolding as expected. I haven't yet received all that I've been prayerfully anticipating.

Now I am in no way diminishing prophetic gifting and prophetic ministry. My life has been and continues to be gloriously formed and directed through the prophetic graces I've received. It's just that there have been and continue to be times and seasons when there's a measure of confusion, or at least uncertainty, when I'm left wondering, "What the hang is going on?"

I have it settled that I'm ok with God working in and through my life far more than I can presently see or understand. (Flip it:

do you only want God to do those things that only make sense to you? My guess is that some of you are nodding, 'Ya, that would be great.' Bless your hearts.)

But I have it sorted that my loving Heavenly Father purposes a destiny for my life that is larger than I will ever be able to comprehend on this side of eternity. With that settled I then have to come to terms with a measure of uncertainty, even confusion. The rub comes when I can't make sense of what God seems to be calling forth.

One response that doesn't serve is anxiety. If, in the face of uncertainty, I get all wound up, indulge in a hissy fit, or worse, throw a little tantrum, that has me self-preoccupied. And self-preoccupation has me living inside a very small and unproductive circle.

Like so many other things, I've learned this the hard way. Years ago, while I was writing *We Dance Because We Cannot Fly*, I got myself into quite a self-preoccupied dither. Without going into details, I had a full-on rant that went something along these lines: "C'mon God. You assigned the project. You've got to give me what I need to finish it." In answer to that 'faith-filled' prayer, the Lord spoke a very clear word: *"You cannot force, and you must not fuss."*

Writing is a gift. It's hard work, but it's a gift. A gift received. The thing is, all of life is a gift. It's hard work, but it's a gift. A gift… received. If we fuss and try to force things, it will never go well. This is not news.

Fussing and forcing is not the exercise of faith. It's us working hard to fix things, in our strength, using our resources, on our timetable. And as I review the course of my life, that has always left me limping.

Grace isn't work. At all. At the end of May, 2013, I was with a dear friend of mine, Simon Ponsonby, in Oxford, England. He'd just published a commentary on Romans and over supper we bored his family to tears nuancing aspects of God's absolute sovereignty and divine initiative, and then followed it with a long discussion about the scandal of particularity, that God chooses to use particular people at particular times in particular places.

As we were clearing the table I asked Simon if he remembered meeting a friend of his in a coffee shop just off the High Street a couple of years earlier. As I recalled, the guy was studying 19th Century romantic poets, and we talked about a sonnet he was reading. I had written a few of the lines in my journal but couldn't find them, and couldn't remember them but felt like they were important for a message I was to preach on that trip.

Simon remembered the meeting and said, "That was Big Tom. He was doing a DPhil in English Lit. I haven't seen him in at least a year. He finished his degree and moved to Cambridge." Simon texted a mate of his, and moments later he wrote down Tom's contact details on a slip of paper, which I put in my pocket. We then headed to the Turf for a little 'cultural exposure.' (The Turf is a terrific old pub in Oxford.) As soon as we rounded the corner onto the heaving High Street, we walked straight into Big Tom.

He and Simon got re-connected, and then Tom recognised me, and remembered our time in the coffee shop. Simon and I had goofy grins on our faces. Not only could we say, "We were just talking about you;" I showed him the slip of paper with his contact details on it.

The three of us were all a little weirded out. I said, "I know it was two years ago, but you were reading a sonnet, something about 'the strength of love.'" Tom shook his head. "It wasn't a sonnet. It was from Wordsworth's poem, *Michael.*" Then he said, "Lines 450-453:

'There is a comfort in the strength of love,
T'will make a thing endurable,
Which else would overset the brain
or break the heart.'"

———•———

There's been quite a measure of uncertainty over my life the last seven years. I basically have had no idea whatsoever as to what was happening with my life. With a very few exceptions, there's been next to nothing in the diary. For most of the time, as far as I could see — there has been nothing on the horizon. Not just ministry. Pick an aspect of my life. Nothing on the horizon that I could see. At times, it has felt irresponsible not to freak out.

But anxiety has not been an option. At least, not a viable one. Trusting abandon has been. Trusting abandon, in the strength of God's unfailing love. Over and against the anxiety that would 'overset my brain and break my heart,' I have known a comfort in the strength of his love that makes the thing endurable. And I receive that time on the High Street with Simon and Tom as a token of exquisite grace.

I have had a lot of prophetic revelation spoken over my life. There's a lot that has yet to be fulfilled. Big stuff. As Paul prayed, "immeasurably more than all I can ask or conceive."[106] So much of the time, I can't see any of it coming round on my horizon. Especially given present circumstances.

But meeting Tom on the Oxford High Street, that exquisite grace, convinces me, again, that as I abandon myself to the Lord's sovereign authority over my life, he has me in exactly the right place, at exactly the right time, with exactly the right people, though I often haven't a clue as to what is going on.

'There is a comfort in the strength of love,
t'will make a thing endurable.'

But there's more to that particular story. Simon and I serendipitously bumped into Tom on the High Street Monday May 27th. The following day, I was with two buddies golfing at the Berkshire. On the fourth tee, I had an overwhelming sense that my life was going to change in fundamental ways on that trip. I had no idea how; I just knew things would not be the same. It was such a strong feeling, I told my buddies. And I was very encouraged. They had that *"O—kayyy... Whatever...."* look on their faces. They also made it clear that they wanted me to hit my tee shot so we could get on with game.

Twelve days later, I had a blind first-date in London that lasted ten hours. And three months later, September 7th, after one exquisite grace followed by another, I asked Kerry if she'd marry me. She said Yes, and three months later we were married, and it's been more than wonderful.

Now, I still don't have a salaried job. But I keep praying, and writing, and waiting. All the while, I continue to meditate on grace. This passage for instance: "I have been crucified with Christ and I no longer live, but Christ lives in me. The life I now live in the body, I live by faith in the Son of God, who loved me and gave himself for me."[107]

We are heirs of the great Protestant Reformation, and Martin Luther's defining strap line, *sola fide*, "faith alone." It's the lens through which we in the West translate the Scriptures, and interpret them, and live them out, like the passage just quoted above. However, the Apostle Paul just said that he had been crucified with Christ. As in, put to death. But that begs the question: how much faith does a dead man have?

When Jesus was standing in front of Lazarus's tomb, did he yell, 'Lazarus, you gotta believe!' No. Lazarus's part was to be a very good corpse. The player in that story was Jesus, the One who said, "I am the Resurrection and the Life. Lazarus, come forth."[108]

Back to Paul's declaration: "I have been crucified with Christ, ... and the life that I now live I live by faith in the Son of God...." In Latin, *sola fide*. *Faith alone*. Sorry, Luther. That translation doesn't make sense, because if I've been crucified with Christ, I'm dead. More importantly, it misses Paul's point. That translation interprets the genitive subjectively — my faith. But I've been crucified with Christ.

When working on this text, Bible translators have to make a choice, whether to interpret things subjectively, or objectively. The question it raises is, Whose faith is at work here? If it were translated objectively, it would read that the "life that I now live, I live by the faithfulness of the Son of God."

There are at least four other times when the Apostle used the phrase that's most often translated subjectively, "by faith," when it holds a great deal more consequence when rendered objectively, as Paul did in Romans: "the righteousness of God... has been disclosed — namely, the righteousness of God through *the faithfulness of Christ* for all who believe."[109] Similarly, in Galatians: "no one is justified by the works of the law, but by *the faithfulness of Christ Jesus*,"[110] and Philippians: "found in [Christ], not because I have my own righteousness derived from the law, but because I have the righteousness that comes by way of *Christ's faithfulness*."[111]

So what? I know that this much grammar causes some readers to slip into a coma. But it is a big deal. There are uncertainties in the living of life. That's a promise to live by. By times it's confusing. By times it's disorientating. By times it's just plain hard. And morning after morning, the alarm clock goes off. If I rehearse all that's ahead, and ask myself, "Do I have enough faith to face the day?" I may well pull the covers over my head and hope it all goes away.

If, instead, I rehearse all that's ahead, and remind myself of the Lord's faithfulness to me, I can throw back the covers, make a strong cup of coffee, and make a beginning. Again.

My faith is not in my faith. My faith is in his faithfulness. And *'there is a comfort in the strength of love, T'will make a thing endurable.'*

Notes

101. Acts 16.1-5
102. Galatians 5.1-3
103. Acts 16.10
104. Mark 16.15, NIV.
105. Acts 16.23
106. Ephesians 3.20
107. Galatians 2.20, NIV.
108. See John 11.25 and 43
109. Romans 3.21-22, NET.
110. Galatians 2.16, NET.
111. Philippians 3.9, NET.

11
SIBERIA OF THE SOUL

Way back in my second year of seminary I came across a book in a friend's library that saved my life. It was a skinny little book by Anthony Bloom, titled *Beginning to Pray*. One of my professors had read a bit of it one morning in chapel. From the swirl of my unconscious, I must have somehow remembered that I was impressed with what the author had to say, and that's why I pulled it from my friend's library. The back cover blurb took my breath away: "The day God is absent, when he is silent, that is the beginning of prayer."

Lest anyone panic, let me clarify at the outset: there are times when we, at least I, sense God's absence. God is, by nature, omnipresent. He is closer to us than we are to ourselves. He is never not present. We have his wonderful promise, "I will never leave you or desert you."[112] But there are times, even seasons, when it feels like the heavens are brass, when it seems that God is deaf to our cries, when we, at least I, feel a terrifying aloneness.

Back to June '78. I was in the midst of one of the hardest times of my life, and what Bloom had written made sense when nothing else did. So much so that at the end of September I withdrew from 2nd year seminary and flew to England. Bloom lived in London. I needed to talk to him. I figured, 'How hard could it be to find a

Russian Orthodox Archbishop in central London?' It only took a month to locate him, and when I sheepishly knocked on his front door he spent two grace-filled hours with me. That time with Bloom was one of the defining moments of my life.

To that point in my walk with God I had lived with the basic, fundamental first principle that he is our Heavenly Father. That presumed his relational immediacy. It presumed that he was not far off, but close at hand. It presumed that he speaks to the likes of us. It presumed that he makes himself, and his will, known to us. I still firmly believe these things, but not so naively.

I've read and re-read Bloom's *Beginning to Pray*, just like I have Anne Lamott's book, *Bird by Bird*, though for very different reasons. Her book is subtitled, "Some Instructions on Writing and Life," and in it she has some outrageous idioms. For instance, she quotes something she heard in a recovery group: "Getting all of one's addictions under control is a little like putting an octopus to bed."[113] That made me think about trying to build a theology and practice of prayer. It too is like putting an octopus to bed, even if it's a reasonably well-behaved octopus. There are just so many big wiggly bits, it isn't easy to get things all tucked in.

One particular wiggly bit goes by various names, always written in capitals, and it has a long history. It's been called simply, The Desert. Or The Wilderness Wanderings. The early Church Fathers spoke of The Hell of Mercy. It's been called The Cloud of Unknowing. Five hundred years ago, John of the Cross coined what became its classic name, though the original Spanish title has a certain mystique that's lost in translation: *La Nocha Oscura del Alma* — The Dark Night of the Soul. Martin Luther contrasted *Deus Revelatus* and *Deus Absconditus*, God Revealed/ God Hidden. Others have called it The Night of the Senses or

The Winter of the Heart. What it's felt like to me is The Siberia of the Soul. Whatever it's called, it is as Anthony Bloom wrote: God experienced as distressingly absent, distressingly silent.

All of this has consistent Scriptural witness. The following verse could serve as a gentle beginning: "The one who walks in dark places with no light, let him trust in the name of the Lord and rely on his God."[114] Things get a little rougher in the Psalms:

Lord, my God, by day I call for help…
hear my loud entreaty;
for I have had my fill of woes,
which have brought me to the brink of Sheol…
You have plunged me into the lowest abyss,
into the darkest regions of the depths…
I am shut in with no escape;
my eyes are dim with anguish…
Lord, why have you cast me off,
why do you hide your face from me?...
You have taken friend and neighbour far from me;
darkness is now my only companion.[115]

Unsettlingly, this is not an obscure, unusual passage. Tally it up, and more than half the Psalms are laments decrying the Lord's sensed absence.

Some would be quick to say, "But that's the Old Testament." If it were only so. In the Gospels, after Jesus was baptised in the Jordan, the heavens opened and there sounded the glorious approbation, "You are my beloved Son; in you I take delight."[116] As Matthew and Luke record the story, Jesus was then *led* into the wilderness.[117] That's a bit unexpected. Right after baptism, why the wilderness, the desert? In Mark's Gospel we're told "the Spirit *drove* him out into the wilderness."[118] That's not just unexpected; I find it disturbing. It feels almost violent. Why would God drive his beloved Son into the wilderness? And which was it — led, or driven? Why don't the Gospel writers agree? Maybe because it's not an either/or, but both/and. Maybe Jesus was led and driven.

While we're writing 'Oh-oh' in the margins of our Bibles, let's continue to nuance things. One glorious summer afternoon I was talking with a pastor about one of my favourite themes, revival, in one of my favourite contexts, a golf course. (Martin Luther contended that the pub was the best place to talk theology. I think it's even better on a golf course.) My pastor-friend asked me, "Why don't revivals last? Why does it lift?" I corrected his syntax. "'It' doesn't lift. Revival, re-viving, is 'coming to life again' by the power and presence of the Spirit of God among, within us. The question should be, 'Why does *he* lift?'" My friend conceded my point.

I don't remember our conversation exactly, but I traced something of the following. Where there's wilful sin, presumptive sin, the Spirit of God absents himself. That's the essence of the prophet's words: "Your eyes are too pure to look on evil."[119] But his lifting is a function of his mercy. If God stayed present while we persist in sin, we would experience the severity of judgment.

Presence is a function of relationship, of openness, vulnerability, and integrity. Almost poetically, the Apostle John put it this way: "God is light, and in him there is no darkness at all. If we claim to be sharing in his life while we go on living in darkness, our words and our lives are a lie. But if we live in the light as he himself is in the light, then we share a common life."[120] In other words, if we're committed to heading in the wrong direction, we won't feel very close to God.

But there are times when wilful sin is not the cause of the

sensed absence. I have long sustained myself with the following prayer by the Trappist monk, Thomas Merton:

My Lord God, I have no idea where I am going. I do not see the road ahead of me. I cannot know for certain where it will end. Nor do I really know myself, and the fact that I think I am following Your will does not mean that I am actually doing so. But I believe that the desire to please You does in fact please You. And I hope I have that desire in all that I am doing. I hope that I will never do anything apart from that desire. And I know that if I do this You will lead me by the right road, though I may know nothing about it. Therefore I will trust You always, though I may seem to be lost and in the shadow of death. I will not fear, for You are ever with me, and You will never leave me to face my perils alone.[121]

Again, there are times when I've felt God's absence, his silence. More than once — ok, quite regularly — I've prayed, "Lord, if there's some reason I can't hear you, please speak to one of the prophetic guys I know, and have them call me."

———•———

Back to the Gospel texts and the Spirit leading Jesus/driving Jesus into the wilderness. There was no sin in Jesus. There was no presumption. Here, the silence, the absence of God, the desert, the dark night, is not a function of sin. Not in Jesus. This, like everything else, is a function of God's love. And love always desires to deepen relationship.

That ought to help us understand our wilderness experiences. Prayer is an encounter, an expression of relationship. Like any relationship, it too is one that cannot be forced. If there was a way we could mechanically make God present to us, if we could force him to meet us, to answer our prayers, it wouldn't be a healthy relationship. Rather, it would be in the realm of magic and witchcraft. Of control. Of power.

But if we try to see our experience through a relational lens, it ought to give us pause when we complain that God does not make himself present to us for the few minutes we devote to our prayer time. What about the twenty-three and a half hours during which he may be calling, knocking at our door and we're busy? The truth of the matter is that most of us are far more absent from God than he ever is from us, even if we pray for longer than half an hour.

In John's Gospel we have the precious invitation of Jesus to intimate, fruitful relationship, to abide in him as he abides in us.[122] We are invited to know him as he knows us, and to bear much fruit. I read that, and I think of one of my favourite outings when I'm privileged to be in Cape Town, South Africa. The wineries in Stellenbosch host some magnificent tours, and on one occasion I was there just before harvest. The vines were nearly collapsing they were so laden with grapes.

But I've also been to that very same vineyard well after harvest, in South African winter, and seen those same vines pruned back such that they looked ravaged. They looked like withered, amputated stumps. I know the feeling. In midst of the Lord's precious invitation to intimate, fruitful relationship in John 15, Jesus made specific mention of pruning. Rightly understood, that should cause us a certain measure of panic. Pruning a grape vine is not a gentle little snip here and there. It's a violent, savage, excessive cutting back, such that all that's left is a stump.

If you've read this far, my guess is that you'd be very grateful to know more of the Lord's gracious presence in your life. You'd be quick to receive his grace unto greater fruitfulness. But when it comes to the pruning... most of us, me included, hope there's another way. The thing is, the witness of the Scriptures and the saints of the Church make it clear that savage, excessive pruning is normative. Every Spirit-guided believer will be led/driven into the wilderness, and probably more than once.

In case you're wondering how this can possibly be a function of God's love, there are aspects of spiritual maturity, and spiritual authority that get sorted only in the desert. Or prison. Often both. Consider the life of Moses. Or Elijah. Jeremiah. Paul. Anthony of Egypt. John of the Cross. Dietrich Bonhoeffer. Nelson Mandela. Each of them spent considerable time in the desert, or prison, or both. I once preached at a conference with a gentleman who moved in great signs and wonders, and over lunch I asked him, "What has your anointing cost you?" He gawked and said, "No one has ever asked me that question, but that's exactly the case, isn't it?"

The Desert doesn't have to be a literal desert or prison. The land of milk and money can just as easily be the context for a circumstantial desert, such as the wilderness of failure. Of suffering: mental, physical, financial, or relational. The Dark Night of humiliation. The Hell of estrangement. The Winter of doubt. The Desert of bereavement and loss. Or a smoothie of the lot. And in the midst of it all, the gnawing, aching sense of God's absence, his silence. With the Psalmist we cry: "Why do you hide your face from me?" WHY?

———•———

Take a deep breath and ready yourselves, because in order to answer the question, I need to talk about the collapse of subject/object dualism. Ready? I'm here, you're there. I'm the subject, the one writing, and you're the object, the one who is hopefully still reading.

Relationship with Jesus starts with a subject/object dualism. We pray; he listens. He speaks; we listen. We have a sense of his presence — we're 'here;' he's 'there.' But in this subject/object dualism, there's still the sense of 'me,' and a sense of 'him.' The children's choir sang about it a couple of Sundays ago:

Teach me Lord Jesus, to be more like you;
gentle and caring in all that I do.
Every day, show me your way,
that I may grow closer to you.
Help me to love like
the way that you do,
pure and unselfish,
humble and true.
Lord I pray, show me your way,
so that I may be more like you.

Beautiful. But… that prayer is based on a subject/object dualism — me, and Jesus. More love, humility, truth, that *I* may be more *like* Jesus.

Recall the Apostle's statement, "I have been crucified with Christ: the life I now live is not my life, but the life which Christ lives in me."[123] This is so much more than a subject/object dualism. This is abiding, also referred to as indwelling, or union. In another of his letters, Paul used God's purpose in marriage, "the two shall become one flesh," as an illustration of this union. He said, "There is hidden here a great truth, which I take to refer to Christ and to the church."[124] In Greek that phrase reads *mysterion touto mega* — a 'mega-mystery.'

Paul's "union" with Christ is what John calls "abiding" in

Christ. Back to the vine and branches. Where does one stop and the other start? The question can't really be answered because both share the same essence, the same sap, the same DNA. By way of the metaphor, it's not so much us becoming more like Christ, and producing nice grapes for Jesus. It is for us to die to self, and find our true selves in him, and his life in us.

This is Kingdom restoration. Pre-fall, Adam and Eve knew a graced harmony with each other, with all of creation, and union with God. In their fall from grace, their perception and experience of reality became dualistic. They experienced separation from God, from each other, and hostility with creation itself.

This brings us back to the Siberia of the Soul. One aspect of the sensed absence of God is unto a further pruning of the ego, the self-absorbed 'I', the demanding 'me' that causes us all manner of grief. The Desert gives us the opportunity to deal with our compulsions, our illusions, and the delusions with which we live. The Dark Night gives us the opportunity to confront our excuses, and what we do with ourselves when everything runs aground. If all of that remains unexplored, if we refuse the gift, those same drives and compulsions become addictions. And distracted by distraction, we distract ourselves to death. And a distracted life has me travelling at ninety miles an hour through an interior wasteland. Time and again, it is only stillness and silence that restore any sense of peace, and hope, and security. As a reminder, I have taped the following quote on my study wall, just to the left of the computer screen:

True encounter with Christ in the Word of God awakens something in the depth of our being, something we did not know was there. True encounter with Christ liberates something in us, a power we did not know we had; a hope, a capacity for life, a resilience, an ability to bounce back when we thought we were completely defeated, a capacity to grow, and change, a power of creative transformation.[125]

Notes

112. Hebrews 13.5
113. Anne Lamott, *Bird by Bird*, p. 93.
114. Isaiah 50.10
115. Psalm 88.1-3,6,9,14,18
116. Mark 1.11
117. Matthew 4.1; Luke 4.2
118. Mark 1.12
119. Habakkuk 1.13
120. 1 John 1.5-9
121. *Thoughts in Solitude,* Farrar, Straus and Giroux, New York: 1956, p. 79.
122. John 15.4
123. Galatians 2.20
124. Ephesians 5.32
125. Thomas Merton, *He Is Risen*, Argus Communications, 1975, p. 15.

12

GRACED TRUTH

If you've never experienced the Lord's sensed absence, don't worry. He has other ways to work his loving grace deep into our lives. 'Deep' is the operative word.

Over the years, I've helped build several houses, and renovated many more. One of the things that taught me is that you have to start building from the bottom up. For instance, if you want to do a loft conversion the first place that needs assessment is not your attic but your foundations, because you cannot build anything that will last without solid foundations.

Imagine that you include a spacious ensuite in your newly renovated loft. Once the work is finally completed, you fill the six-foot Roman bathtub to the brim, ease yourself into the steamy hot water, and you breathe a deep, satisfied sigh of relief. The whole thing has been far more of a project than you ever imagined. You splash about a bit, and then you hear a very loud crack... and then an extending groaning sort of noise. Shortly thereafter you and the tub crash through the floor. The reason: there wasn't enough support underneath.

Over the years, I've assessed the structural integrity of over fifty houses. Some of them have been done up very smartly, and many have been decorated with real flair. Some have been very functional, yet very comfortable. I look beyond all that. If there are cracks in the corners of the walls, if the doors don't shut properly, if the floors list to starboard, I know that regardless of how good the place may look, there are foundational troubles that haven't been dealt with. Somebody has painted over some very serious problems.

I've had to tell several homeowners that their house had structural issues. It's never been fun, for either of us. I've shown them the problems — crumbling foundations, sagging beams, rotted-out posts. There's always a hang-dog look that pleads for a simple, easy solution: "Couldn't you just....?" I have a standard answer. "Do you really want me to put a bandaid on this malignant cancer?" It may take them a while, but eventually most of them have asked, "What do we need to do to fix it?"

In the renovation business there's a mantra that runs, "All it takes is time and money." Given enough of both, I've yet to encounter a problem that can't be fixed, even the most structural, foundational ones. They've just required a lot of digging.

———•———

Spiritually, our foundations are cracked. That's the assessment the Apostle Paul brought in the Book of Romans. After a brief review of human history, he made a categorical declaration: "All have sinned."[126] Something's heaved, something's shifted, and there's something fundamentally wrong in each and every one of us. Try this: after a moment's reflection, there would be very few of us who would dispute the fact that anger makes you stupid. The majority of us know this the hard way. At some time or another, we've lost our temper and done something, or at least said something that we later regretted. Probably more than once. If I asked for a show of hands, it would include almost all of us.

If it doesn't include you, how about a show of hands for those that are liars? We are all diseased — dis-eased. We do not live in perfect peace. We all live something short of wholeness, and holiness.

The Good News is that in Christ, we are being restored. Jesus brings re-creation. In him we experience new creation, such that the old passes away. As yet, our individual experience of this redemptive process is incomplete. While we are no longer what we were, we are not yet all that we shall be. We await the new heaven and the new earth, when there will be no more suffering, no more sickness, no more pain. Until then, there's a groaning both in our own heart of hearts, and in creation itself.

Some of us are more acutely aware of this than others, but in each and every one of us there are longings — for healing, for freedom, for deliverance — from that which causes in us dis-ease. There is in most of us, a longing for restoration.

———·———

In the first chapter of this book, we considered the divine order to God's redemptive work: grace precedes truth.[127] When that order is inverted, when truth trumps grace, many of us have been subjected to a certain brutality 'in the name of Jesus.' Graceless truth is exclusive, judgemental, and usually wounding. Truthless grace, however, is not the solution. It may be inclusive, and tolerant, but there's little that leads to repentance and the transformation of a distorted life.

It would be so much easier if it were grace *or* truth. If we could decide which of the two seemed to be most needed in a given situation, which of the two would best solve a particular problem, which of the two we were most gifted in, then we could merrily attempt to fix whatever seemed problematic. But it ought never be an either/or choice, grace or truth, to the exclusion of the other.

Grace and truth are ever to be held together in restorative tension. Repeatedly, I've posed the question, 'Where's grace in this?' Without diminishing the redemptive consequences of grace in any way, the question 'Where's truth in this?' must also be asked.

Holding these two questions in continuous tension isn't easy for any of us, so let's go round the block one more time. What distinguished the love of Jesus was that he cared for people which society, especially the religious, said were the wrong people to love. Jesus was, and is, the "friend of sinners." Full stop. He doesn't maintain a list — the friend of adulterers, gluttons, embezzlers, gossips and drunks — but if your sin doesn't make it on the list, he's not willing to be your friend. No. He extends unqualified, unconditional acceptance and friendship to each and every one of us, no exceptions. His is an unconditional inclusivity, irrespective of our behaviour, good or bad.

If we want to be like Jesus — more, if with the Apostle Paul, we want to live a unified life such that it is no longer we who live but Christ who lives in us, then we too will be the friend of sinners. Full stop. No list. God has no favourites. Nor should we.

As church, we ought to be the most inclusive of all organisations, demonstrating a committed, courageous and compassionate inclusion of those who, for whatever reason, find themselves marginalised.

That's Job One. But it's not our only job. While unconditionally inclusive, and unconditionally accepting, we are also a people who are called to an ongoing process of transformation. Not just change for change sake, or any old change. In Christ, we are a people committed to sanctification. We all come "Just as we are," but we're not to stay that way. We are not meant to continue living the mess we've made of life. We have a new life that is so much bigger, and freer, and fuller than our old life.

While it's not made explicit in the Book of Acts, this transformation is clearly evidenced. A disciple called Ananias extended unconditional inclusion to a murderer named Saul. The Holy Spirit sent him to pray for the man. Ananias obediently went and found him, laid his hands on him, and spoke grace-filled words over him: "Saul, my brother …."[128]

Thereafter, Saul was unconditionally accepted by the fellowship of believers, though there were some in the gathering who were, understandably, a little nervous. While Saul was unconditionally accepted, his past behaviour was not endorsed. He was not encouraged to keep on murdering Christians. On the contrary, Saul's life was so transformed that he became the Apostle of Love.

Like Saul, we are each a product of three natures: our created nature, our fallen nature, and our redeemed nature in Christ. In each of us, there is what we were made and meant to be, what's been mashed and marred, and what's being made new. At the deepest, truest core of our being, our identities are given in both creation and redemption. It is ours then to choose to align, to agree with what God purposes, and so engage in the restoration of our fallen nature, the transformation of all that's been mashed and marred.

In his first letter to the church in Corinth, the Apostle Paul named some aspects of fallen nature, and how this fallenness manifests: there are the sexually immoral, idolaters, adulterers, male prostitutes and homosexual offenders, thieves, the greedy, drunkards, slanderers and swindlers.[129] It is a comprehensive list, but not an exhaustive one. It is descriptive, rather than definitive. Paul might as well have asked, 'Did I miss anyone?'

But it wasn't Paul's purpose to whack the Corinthians for the particulars of their sinful behaviour. His concern was just the opposite: he wrote to help them understand what it means to belong to "the church of God... those sanctified in Christ Jesus and called to be his holy people." That's the way Paul introduced the letter.[130] What he named was the deep transformation and change of lifestyle that comes by way of redemption and restoration. Paul then addressed habituated fallen behaviour. Eugene Peterson puts it well in his paraphrase: "A number of you know from experience what I'm talking about, for not so long ago you were on that list."[131]

Let's work through things here, because as diverse as Paul's list may seem, there is a common thread holding it all together. "Sexual immorality." The original Greek word is *porneia*, a general term for immorality. It's used to refer to any sexual relations outside of marriage. Then Paul turned things time and again. "Idolatry" is taking hold of, and being held, not by the Creator, but by a creature or the created. "Adultery" is taking hold of someone else's spouse; sex with someone else's spouse. *Malakoi kai arsenokoitai.* The NIV translates the phrase as "male prostitutes and homosexuals." A literal translation would read 'the passive male partners' and 'the dominant male partners.' In this context, 'the man who is held' and 'the man who holds.' That's as explicit as we'll get in this forum. *Kleppti*, "thieves," those who steal what isn't theirs. "The greedy," literally grasping more than is one's lawful due. It is not unrelated to adultery; both take what isn't rightfully theirs. "Drunkards," those who take too long and too strong a hold on the bottle – and let the bottle have too strong a hold on them. "Slanderers," those who have no hold on their tongues; "Swindlers," those whom money has in a stranglehold.

And none of them will "possess the kingdom of God."[132] Paul's conclusion sounds exclusive. It sounds judgemental. At face value that doesn't sound like Good News, but it is. A little interactive interpretation helps us to understand. Make a fist. As long as you insist on holding tight, what can you receive? Keep on grasping, and you can't 'take hold' of the Kingdom.

"Such were some of you." While fallen nature characterised life before knowing the power of Christ's love, it is no longer determinative. There has come a graced release from the grasping. There's no longer the need to try to hang on to that which will not give life. Those things no longer control our lives. Paul reminded the church, "You have been washed clean, you have been dedicated to God, you have been justified through the name of the Lord Jesus and through the Spirit of our God."[133]

That last phrase is key: "through the Spirit of our God." Twenty-five years ago, I built an addition on a friend's house. His twelve-year old son was helping us. Late one afternoon I heard him say to his dad, "Guy sure is manic with his spirit-level, isn't he?" We were putting up the walls that day. Yes, I was manic with my spirit-level.

If I put up walls that aren't absolutely vertical, if I go with what 'feels right,' I'll have serious structural problems. Does a spirit-level limit my freedom? Yes, in that it keeps me from building any which way I feel like. But it alone enables strong, structurally sound construction. It is an absolute I cannot compromise without destructive consequence. 'Close enough; good enough; that'll do' all make for shoddy building practices.

Now perhaps the biggest zinger in this book: spiritually, what is that absolute? In restoring our foundations, and transforming our lives, what are the absolutes that cannot be compromised without destructive consequence? There was a time when I would have quickly and unhesitatingly answered, 'The Bible.'

But my faith is not in the Bible. My faith is in the One to whom the Scriptures witness. My relationship is with Jesus, as he reveals the Father, under the inspiration of the Holy Spirit.

Back to the Apostle Paul's list cited above. To make the particulars on that list the focus of concern — sexual immorality, idolatry, homosexuality, drunkenness, greed — or any particular sin that's not on the list —is to go with 'what feels right — or wrong.' The absolute is that which the Holy Spirit is calling forth, unto the redemption and restoration of a *particular* life. That will very often be revealed in and through the Scriptures, either as they are meditated upon privately, or listened to when preached. But we don't have a relationship with the Bible. We relate to the One who reveals the Bible to us.

I became a Christian at eighteen. Sexually, I was behaving much like a tomcat. But in those early months after my conversion, the Holy Spirit didn't convict me about my sexual immorality. Rather, it was my speeding.

At the time, I rode a 500cc Honda motorcycle, and all its horsepower called out to be exercised. Prior to my conversion, I fantasised about suicide frequently, and I rode accordingly. I regularly put myself at risk. After I gave my life to the Lord, I was reading the Scriptures every day. But there are no "Thou shalt not speed" verses in the Bible. The only thing that comes anywhere close is a passing reference to one of Israel's kings: "His driving is like that of Jehu son of Nimshi — he drives like a maniac."[134] But that didn't change my heart. Rather, it was the Holy Spirit's stirring unto life. As in, staying alive. The conviction he brought to my heart was an absolute I could not compromise without destructive consequence.

Characteristically, that's how the Holy Spirit prioritises graced conviction. What is at work in our lives that most steals life? What most distorts life? What most compromises the fullness the Lord purposes for us? While we all have issues, the Holy Spirit doesn't deal first and foremost with 'issues.' There's no person in an issue. An issue is a philosophical, sociological, political, psychological problem.

Consider someone who has anger issues. Let's say that it doesn't take much for them to erupt. They and their family continuously have to deal with the wreckage that ensues. There's a great deal of truth in the statement: 'Over-reaction points to a wounding every time.' Yes, the one going ballistic has anger issues. But what's the unhealed wounding that is so raw it doesn't take much to cause such an over-reaction?

We could implement all sorts of clever anger management strategies and try to address the issues, but unless and until the deep-core wounding is sorted, it's like suggesting this person try to hold a beachball underwater. Sooner or later, that thing is going to pop to the surface again.

Instead, think of the Holy Spirit as a very discerning building inspector. You finally get to the place where you want to deal with your anger issues. You ask for his help. He doesn't look at your anger issues first and foremost. He starts with your foundations. He points out what's shifted, what's heaved, what's rotted and crumbled. And you ask, weakly, "Couldn't you just...?" He asks, "Do you really want me to put a bandaid on this malignant cancer?" This is the moment where you courageously respond, "What do we need to do to fix it?"

Notes
126. Romans 3.23, NIV.
127. John 1.14
128. Acts 9.17
129. 1 Corinthians 6.9-11
130. 1 Corinthians 1.2, NIV.
131. 1 Corinthians 6.11, The Message.
132. 1 Corinthians 6.10
133. 1 Corinthians 6.11
134. 2 Kings 9.20, NIV.

13

THE WAY ON

There are times when we don't ask what needs fixing. Ready or not, it gets pointed out for us. But it doesn't always go the graced way the Apostle Paul said it should: "If anyone is caught doing something wrong, you, my friends, who live by the Spirit must gently set him right."[135] It would be very easy to tell all manner of stories when that hasn't quite been the case. Many of us know this first-hand. We've been caught doing something wrong and were "set right" in no uncertain terms. Our 'friends' were anything but gentle.

Miracle Max, from *The Princess Bride*, could speak for many of us when he lamented, "Thank you *so* much for bringing up such a painful subject. While you're at it, why don't you give me a paper cut and pour lemon juice on it?" Paper cuts are one thing. No doubt there are some readers whose graceless woundings are such that they are struggling to hold back the tears.

Yet there are glorious exceptions. I know of a church leader who fell spectacularly. He stole from the church; he stepped out on his wife and abandoned his children, and he returned to the drugs that had ravaged his life. Those were the headlines.

For almost a year, he was a living train-wreck. Then one Sunday he braved a return to his church. One of the other leaders saw him walk in. They immediately left the person they had been talking to and made a bee-line straight for him. As they approached, they called him by name. With wide-open arms, they enfolded him and as tears ran down their face they whispered in his ear, "We were so afraid we'd lost you. We love you so much." Over the next two years, his church nurtured him as his life was resurrected, and gradually he was restored to leadership where he serves with a profound humility, gratitude and authority.

'You who live by the Spirit must gently set the sinner right.' That admonition was addressed to the church, for those in the church. The Apostle Paul was well-aware that there are times when we — in the church — all get it wrong. We all need someone to come alongside and gently help us to find our way again. 'Gently' is the word that hopefully gets underlined.

Just so there's no misunderstanding, a heavy-handed, highly controlling and fault-finding response is anything but the gentleness Paul had in mind. When he confronted the Corinthian church, he made the contrast crystal-clear: "Shall I come to you with a rod of discipline, or shall I come in love and with a gentle spirit?"[136] One lays down the Law with a rod of discipline; one exercises grace and truth with a gentle spirit.

Both the parable of the lost sheep and the parable of the prodigal son illustrate what gentle restoration looks like. The sheep who wandered away was previously part of the flock. In the spirit of inclusion, let's say that the sheep in question was a female. She belonged. She was 'in.' She just got careless. She got distracted. She made a series of dumb decisions.[137]

Before he left home and made a complete mess of his life, the prodigal was a privileged son, beloved of his father. He belonged. He too, was 'in.' And so much more so than the sheep, he wilfully, rebelliously turned his back and walked away from all that he had.[138] Both the lost sheep and the lost boy were lovingly, graciously, gently restored to the flock and the family respectively. Were they under another Covenant, they would have received the rod of discipline, for they both deserved to be beaten senseless. Both of them knew better.

I think it was the theologian Reinhold Niebuhr who said sin is "unnecessary but inevitable." We all make bad choices by times, but it could always be otherwise. So when (not if) someone sins, we can read the riot act to them because they failed to measure up. We can wield the rod of discipline to bring them into line. This we can do all on our own. We know what's right, and we know they're wrong.

The Apostle Paul spoke of another way, and he addressed it to those "who live by the Spirit." In exactly the same situation, faced with exactly the same wrongdoing, it's no longer a 'one on one' confrontation. Those who live by the Spirit are called to relational discernment. It's not just the immediate failure that requires our attention. The Holy Spirit is present. What is he calling forth here? How is the Spirit at work in the midst of this situation? What does he purpose to heal, to restore, to redeem? Answering these sorts of questions sends us to the secret place, not the rule book.

Think for a moment about the difference between church policies, and church guidelines. Many churches have a policy that states, 'A couple has to date for at least a year before they can get married.' That's considered to be good pastoral wisdom, especially for those who are teenage hopefuls. But where's graced discernment in that? We can make that ruling all on our own. It's clean, it's tidy, it's the same for everybody, and it's pastorally pragmatic. If there are no exceptions to the rule, it protects leadership from any potential fallout.

If, instead, it is a church guideline, it's still good pastoral wisdom. But it's only a guideline. A commitment to relational discernment means we suspend our judgements and ask what the Lord is purposing with each couple who present themselves. How is the Spirit at work in their lives? What is he calling forth, and when? The guideline applies to all, but discernment is required for each.

While marriage policy is not a sin situation, take living by the Spirit and the same relational discernment, and bring it to bear in 'gently setting the sinner right.' Imagine you've been 'caught,' and you've been called before your church leadership. The details of your wrongdoing are all exposed — anger, lust, gossip, gluttony, drunkenness, greed, anxious fear — pick your favourite failure. What do you most need to hear from them? What word will help you redeem your mess and transform your life: 'Stop it. Thou shalt not' or 'How's that working for you? What's it costing you?'

Repeatedly we read in the Gospels that Jesus came alongside a person and "had compassion" on them.[139] He didn't use the rod of discipline on the adulterous, the thieving, the arrogant, the angry or the unwell. Jesus "knew what was in each person."[140] It was as if the Gospel were a thousand piece jigsaw puzzle, with the whole made up of the complex of work, and marriage, money, truth, spirituality, sexuality, health, freedom, and peace. He discerned which particular piece was most needed to put an individual life together, and graciously offered that. His compassion gently set them right.

———•———

My mother used to live north of Toronto. When I would go in to visit her, I would get off Highway 401 at the Bayview exit.

Once, while waiting for the traffic lights to change, I watched a young man with a crutch and a paper cup working the queue of cars that had backed up on the exit ramp. It looked like he'd been living rough for some time. I rolled down my window, called him over, and gave him a handful of change. By then the traffic lights had turned green and I had to go.

I can still see the cardboard sign that hung around his neck: *Homeless and hungry, broken and broke. Please help. God bless.* I count that a succinct, articulate, even poetic description of the human condition. A life without the fullness of the Holy Spirit.

We all need help. We all need the blessing of God. Not that I'm encouraging you to wear a cardboard sign around your neck, but reflect on your own life. *Homelessness.* In your heart of hearts, is there yet a longing for belonging? A longing to know a safe place, where you are honoured, and nurtured, and respected? *Hunger.* Is there yet a dissatisfaction, a boredom, an indifference that gnaws away at your soul? *Brokenness.* Anything of an un-healed, un-redeemed woundedness in your life? Anything in your life that doesn't quite work the way you need it to? *Broke.* Do you feel you are able to access all the resources you need to live an abundant and fruitful life? Is there a longing deep within to know more of the power of God's love?

Homeless and hungry, broken and broke. The Apostle James said, "My friends, if one of you strays from the truth and another succeeds in bringing him back, you may be sure of this: the one who brings a sinner back from his erring ways will be rescuing a soul from death and cancelling a multitude of sins."[141]

Please help. But do it gently. *God bless.*

Notes

135. Galatians 6.1
136. 1 Corinthians 4.21, NIV.
137. See Luke 15.3-7
138. See Luke 15.11-13
139. See Mark 1.41, Luke 7.13, Matthew 20.34
140. John 2.25, NIV.
141. James 5.19-20

14
ALL HANDS ON DECK

———•———

Kerry and I were recently at a most remarkable church. They had over *forty* different nations represented in their congregation. After the morning service, we went out for lunch with the church's five elders. The seven of us were from seven different countries, six different continents. (Antarctica was woefully under-represented.)

Over the course of our conversation, I praised the elders for the amazing job they had done in gathering such an internationally eclectic congregation. It was phenomenal the way they'd been able to blend race, and language, and culture. I then looked at the guys and said, "For all your inclusivity, there's only one pretty face at this table." (Lest there be any misunderstanding, I looked in Kerry's direction.) Then I asked, "Why are there no gifted women on your leadership team?"

———•———

I could have asked those elders, 'Where's grace in keeping gifted women from leadership?' but at the time, the question would have been too blunt. I made but a gentle beginning with them. The same is true of this chapter; it is but a gentle beginning.

In the great sweep of the Scriptures, there are three controlling movements, classically named as Creation, Fall, and Redemption.

Those are theological terms that may or may not have meaning and content. If they don't, think: Beginnings, Distortion, and Restoration. To clarify further, these three movements encompass what and how God made and meant things to be; how things have gone wrong; and how he is at work making all things new.

Let's start at the beginning, with the Creation account, and look at what and how God made and meant things to be. Firstly, humankind is made "in the image of God."[142] Secondly, God is relationship: "God said, 'Let *us* make humankind in *our* image....'"[143] God is one essence, but three beings: Father, Son and Holy Spirit. Each of the Three are Godhead in entirety, complete in themselves, yet essentially related. They are distinct, yet complementary. Theirs is a differentiated union.

As image bearers, humankind's essence is also relational. This is nuanced in the next verse: "God created human beings in his own image; in the image of God he created them; male and female he created them."[144] In terms of the creation account, human beings uniquely bear the image of God as no other creature does. And God's image is seen in "them," male and female, in this distinct differentiation, not in 'him' or 'her' alone. In other words, we also are made — created — for relationship. Further: "God blessed them."[145] There is no indication of any superiority of one sex over the other. There is no male hierarchy in the creation account, no privileged position, no indication of subordination. Both male and female are given the authority of stewardship over created order. Both male and female receive the same blessing unto fruitfulness. And this was all "very good."[146]

The second chapter of Genesis is a re-telling of the story of beginnings. It is a complementary, rather than contradictory account of the story. It adds further detail to the creation story. In it, God breathed life into the man-creature he had created, and as it's recorded he is the only creature to be called forth in this way.[147] It's a particularly elegant way of saying that at least in God's eyes, we're in a class of our own. It says that there is something of spirit that is essential to being human. The French theologian Teillard de Chardin expressed it this way: "We are not human beings having brief spiritual experiences; we are spiritual beings having a brief human experience." As humans, the spirit is the determining element of our essential being; diminish our sense of spirit, and we lose our sense of being fully, truly human.

In Genesis 2.18, God created "a helper suitable for the man." The Hebrew word for "helper" is the same one that's used repeatedly when God is named as Helper, as in, "The Lord is our help and our shield."[148] But it begs the question: how was Eve to help Adam? It's not specified. The only thing that's recorded is that she had theological conversations with a snake, and they didn't prove to be all that helpful.

It's here the 'Role of men and women' debate heats up. One early observation: nearly all that I've read on the subject works off a static understanding of role, and most of it is undistinguished from essence.

To clarify, I have two adult children, Graham and Caitlin. Part of my essential nature is that I am their father. You don't fully know me until you know me as their father, because being their father is such a big, essential part of my life. As their father, my role has changed throughout their lives. I had the role of procreator twice. My role as nappy changer, thankfully, lasted about four and a half years. My role as coach's helper in little league baseball lasted five seasons. My role now is one of adult friend, and sometimes wise counsellor. All are essential aspects of my fatherhood, but those different roles have been transitionally determined by need.

To blur essential mutuality (male and female equality) and

differentiated roles (a sexist division of labour), and to impose the subordination and submission of women to men based on this 'helper' text is to contradict their essential equality as it is declared back in the first creation account.[149]

Further, in the second creation account, man has no part in the creation of woman other than donating a spare-rib.[150] She, just as much as he, owes her life to God. Woman was created 'from the side,' not above or below. Over two hundred years ago Matthew Henry put the issue beautifully: "The woman was made out of the side of Adam; not made out of his head to rule over him; nor out of his feet to be trampled upon; but out of his side to be equal with him; under his arm to be protected, and near to his heart to be beloved."[151]

What "near to his heart to be beloved" looks like is spelled out in the following verses: "A man leaves his father and mother and attaches himself to his wife, and the two become one."[152] Notice the order here. Contrary to later cultural patriarchy where men ruled, there is in God's original design an implicit mutuality. In terms of family of origin, both father and mother are named without hierarchical distinction. Further, it's the man who is to leave his family in order to unite with his wife, not the other way round. Because he loves her so much, because he doesn't want to live without her, he is willing to break the closest of family ties and leave everything behind in order to be one with her.

While all this was "very good," it didn't last long. Things got distorted. The third chapter of Genesis sketches the Fall, and in it, the serpent addressed Eve. Why her and not Adam? Subordinationists (yes, that's what they like to call themselves) posit that Eve was the more gullible of the two. As a woman, hers was the "greater propensity to be deceived." Further, subordinationists assert that Satan went behind Adam's back in an attempt to undermine his role as male head. I quote: "The Genesis temptation is a parable of what happens when male leadership is abrogated." Big word, abrogated. Its literal meaning means to do away with a law, to repeal a law, to over-rule. Their argument runs as follows: Eve took the initiative, and Adam complied with her subversion, following her lead. This is then the first of all catastrophic sex role reversals....

But the whole notion of subordination fundamentally contradicts what the first two chapters of Genesis clearly convey. Eve did not tempt Adam. The serpent alone did the tempting. Both Eve and Adam succumbed. Both were culpable. And to blame one over the other misses the essential point of the story.

The temptation hinges on Adam and Eve's relationship with God, and what he said to them, specifically with respect to the tree of the knowledge of good and evil. After Eve had her little discourse with the serpent, she "looked at the tree: the fruit would be good to eat; it was pleasing to the eye and desirable for the knowledge it could give."[153] Recall the earlier chapter: humans alone are God-breathed.[154] We alone are spirit creatures. That's what it means for us to live both the image and likeness of God.

The issue, for all of us, is whether spirit will rule over soul. The temptation — Adam and Eve's — and ours ever after, is to flip that around. To allow fleshly appetite to rule. To live like a spirit-less animal. So the temptation: 'Are you hungry? Eat. Do whatever feels good.'

But to live like a spirit-less animal compromises our essential nature, and the man and woman bear the consequences of their wilful disobedience. Adam ever after must earn his bread by the sweat of his brow.[155] He is now subject to that from which he was taken. And Eve? "Your desire will be for your husband, and he will rule over you."[156] She is now subject to him from whom she was taken. This rule or mastery is a dysfunctionally distorted dynamic to their relationship. As consequence, it implies that man did not rule over woman as they were originally created. The pre-fall mutuality was marred; now, there was no longer a co-equal stewardship over creation; now there was discord, and dispute over power and control. Where God purposed that the two rule over creation as one, they now attempt to rule over each other.

So far, we've sketched Creation, and Distortion; now the third movement — Restoration. It is prophetically foretold, and declared by the Apostle Peter at Pentecost. God purposes to restore all that separates, and divides, and alienates his God-breathed, image bearing creation. God says, "I will pour out my Spirit on all mankind (in it's context, the racial differences of Jew and Gentile are to be transcended); "your sons and daughters shall prophesy (gender differences are transcended); "your young men shall see visions, and your old men shall dream dreams (age differences are transcended). "[I will pour out my Spirit] on my servants and my handmaids" (class distinctions are transcended).[157]

Just so there's no confusion about the word 'transcended,' it means 'to rise above, to go beyond the limits of something.' The differences of nationality, culture, gender, age and class still exist within the church. We all come with history. But in Christ, by his Spirit, we rise above the differences of nationality, culture, gender, age and class. We transcend those differences, and honour one another, prefer one another, and serve one another, well beyond what previously limited and constrained us.

All of this is mirrored in the Apostle Paul's great Restoration declaration: In Christ, "there is no such thing as Jew or Greek, slave and freeman, male or female."[158] As things are restored in

Christ, it's a level playing field. There are to be no distinctions —
not culture, or colour, or class; not age, not even gender. In Christ,
no one has a privileged position. No one has superior status. No
one has special advantage. Each and every one of us gets to play
for one reason and one reason alone — and his name is Jesus.

So far, things have been fairly free and breezy. Now, the two 'What
about…' texts, the texts that kept gifted women from leadership
positions in the church I introduced at the start of this chapter.
What about the text that says, "A woman should learn in quietness
and full submission. I do not permit a woman to teach or to have
authority over a man; she must be silent."[159]

My, my, my. Before moving on, a quick word to those
who insist on taking these verses literally and as if they do so
without interpretation. Consistency and integrity require that
you also take passages in the same letter literally and without
interpretation. If you claim that the Scriptures are to be taken at
face-value, that issues of context and culture shouldn't complicate
what God's Word clearly states, are you as passionate about paying
your pastor a double stipend[160] as you are in prohibiting women
from teaching? In case you don't know what a stipend is, think
of your annual salary. Are you happy to double that by way of
your pastor's salary? (In a public forum, there is usually a bit of
harrumphing and floor-staring at this point in the proceedings.)

In understanding this 'what about' women keeping silent text,
the first question to ask is, Where's grace in that? And once asked,
it should cause us to answer slowly. Taken at face value, these
verses are exclusive, heavy-handed and pejorative. These verses
contradict the relational equality that God originally purposed,
and which he purposes to restore in Christ.

In proceeding, a second question helps: In the three movements of Scripture, where does that text fit? Creation? No. Restoration? Definitely not. There's no transcendence there. We're out of options. This text is in the Distortion section of Scripture.

Let's plod on. Not permitting a woman to teach or have authority over a man directly contradicts God's Creation purpose, and the male and female mutuality and a co-equal stewardship over the created order. It contradicts the Restoration of God's creation purposed in Christ. It also directly contradicts the specific references to the Church's teaching ministry as detailed in three places in the New Testament.[161] None of those passages exclude women. What is emphasised is ministry exercised in giftedness — and the gifts of the Spirit are given irrespective of gender — again, the Spirit is "poured out on all flesh."

To a congregation of both men and women, the Apostle Paul said, "Let the gospel of Christ dwell in you richly as you teach and admonish one another with all wisdom."[162] Grammatically, the pronouns are plural inclusives: as in, 'you all.' He encouraged both men and women to pray and prophecy in church, and he encouraged their mutual submission to one another.[163] He made this explicit earlier: "in the Lord, woman is not independent of man, nor is man independent of woman."[164] Rather, all can prophecy, and all can pray in tongues.[165] He said, "When you come together, everyone has a hymn, or a word of instruction, a revelation, a tongue or an interpretation."[166] In a following verse he said, "You can all prophesy, one at a time, so that all may receive instruction and encouragement."[167]

Over and against this graced and gifted inclusivity irrespective of gender, we suddenly face one heck of a speed bump: "A woman should learn in quietness and full submission. I do not permit a woman to teach or to have authority over a man; she must be silent."[168]

This is no a random attempt at traffic calming. It's there for good reason. At the start of his letter to Timothy, the Apostle Paul got straight down to business, foregoing the usual greetings and encouragement that characterise most of his other letters. He reminded Timothy of why he left him in Ephesus: he was to "instruct certain people to give up teaching erroneous doctrines," those who had "gone astray into a wilderness of words."[169] Paul brought further indictment: those people "set out to be teachers of the law," (note: law, not Gospel) "although they do not understand either the words they use or the subjects about which they are so dogmatic."[170]

Paul intimately knew of Timothy's situation. As recorded in the Book of Acts, Paul had been in Ephesus for a short first visit, and preached in the local synagogue.[171] A Jew named Apollos followed after him, and continued to teach the way of the Lord[172] though he didn't quite have the full story. The local elders, Priscilla (a woman) and Aquila, took him in hand "and expounded the way to him in greater detail."[173]

Paul then returned to Ephesus some time later,[174] and ministered to a gathering of people who had not received any Holy Spirit teaching or ministry. The Apostle stayed with them for three years, and they witnessed not just signs and wonders, but "extraordinary miracles."[175] They did so in the midst of strong opposition, for there were those who were "obdurate… speaking evil of the new way."[176] One of the reasons for the open antagonism was that many of those who had become believers were previously from an occult background, and their conversion more than stirred the spiritual pot, "giving rise to a serious disturbance."[177] Demetrius the silversmith had vested interest at stake, as did others whose livelihood depended on cult industry;[178] his protests were such that he nearly incited the mob to riot. Shortly thereafter, Paul left for Macedonia. But he maintained close contact with the church in Ephesus. Several months later, he sent for their elders.[179] Paul's counsel to them is recorded, as is his warning: "I know that when I am gone, savage wolves will come in among you and will not spare the flock."[180] There will be those who will try to "distort the truth in order to get the disciples to break away and follow them."[181] This was not a new problem in Ephesus: he lamented, "with tears I never ceased to warn each one of you night and day — for three years."[182]

As recorded in the New Testament, no other church was so antagonistic as Ephesus. Paul challenged the Corinthians about their elitism and their arrogance,[183] and in frustration reproved the Galatians for their "foolishness,"[184] but nowhere else spoke so candidly about the opposition he faced "fighting those wild beasts at Ephesus."[185] Nowhere else does Paul caution with the likes of: "Alexander the coppersmith did me great harm... you had better be on your guard against him, for he is bitterly opposed to everything we teach."[186]

That recognised, there are no female troublemakers explicitly named in any of Paul's asides. But recall the over-riding concern Paul addressed in the letter: there were those in Ephesus who taught "erroneous doctrines," which he characterised in two ways: they focused on the law, and they called forth devotion to myths and endless genealogies.[187] Later in his letter, he again warned, "Have nothing to do with superstitious myths, mere old wives' tales."[188]

Paul also devoted considerable attention to the problems that the Ephesian widows were creating for the church. Some of these women were "given to self-indulgence,"[189] and some of the young widows were "worse than idle," given to gossip and busy-bodying, "speaking of things better left unspoken."[190] Paul's recommendation that they get married and bear children[191] was corrective counsel for those who have "forsaken the faith and surrendered their minds to subversive spirits and demon-inspired doctrines."[192] He named two of those doctrines: the forbidding of marriage, and abstinence from certain foods.[193]

With all of this pieced together, might it have been that a considerable group of women were deceived by the false teachers and were spreading those teachings in the church, unduly triumphing the rejection of marriage and childbearing. This would explain why Paul used an unusual word in the 'speed bump' passage, the only time it is used in the New Testament. While the NIV reads that a woman is not "to assume authority over a man,"[194] the word is not *exousia*, the usual Greek word for authority, but a word which means 'to give orders.' Other translations reflect this difference: women must not "usurp authority over the man,"[195] "dictate to the men."[196] Peterson's paraphrase makes the difference clear: "don't let women take over and tell men what to do."[197]

———•———

There's another 'What about…' text: "As in all the congregations of the Lord's people, women should remain silent in the churches. They are not allowed to speak, but must be in submission, as the law says…. It is disgraceful for a woman to speak in the church."[198] It too reads as a blatant contradiction of the inclusive giftedness irrespective of gender that Paul detailed just two chapters earlier in the same letter.[199]

Note that the passage is in a section where Paul addressed problems that the Corinthian church were having with the inappropriate and immature expression of prophetic gifting. Regarding those whose conduct was out of line, Paul said, "they are to keep silent." He does so three times.[200]

The women who are to keep silent may well have been the wives of those who were prophesying, perhaps inappropriately. Regardless, if a man is prophesying and his wife doesn't understand — or agree with — what he is saying, she is not to interrupt him but should wait quietly and patiently until she can ask her husband at home. That's wise counsel, both for the church family, and the marriage.

————•————

The title of this chapter is "All Hands on Deck." Given how great the need, shame on those who insist on playing with only half a deck.

Notes

142. Genesis 1.26
143. Ibid.
144. Genesis 1.27
145. Genesis 1.28
146. Genesis 1.31
147. Genesis 2.7
148. See Psalm 115.9
149. Genesis 1.26-7
150. Genesis 2.21
151. Matthew Henry, *Exposition of all the Books of the Old and New Testaments, vol 1*, Edinburgh, Bell and Bradfute, 1797, p. 26.
152. Genesis 2.24
153. Genesis 3.6
154. Genesis 2.7
155. Genesis 3.19
156. Genesis 3.16, NIV.
157. See Joel 2.28 and Acts 2.17
158. Galatians 3.28
159. 1 Timothy 2.11-12, NIV, 1984. In the 2011 revision, the translators changed "silent" to "quiet."
160. 1 Timothy 5.17-18
161. Romans 12.7, 1 Corinthians 12.4-11 and 27-29, Ephesians 4.11-13
162. Colossians 3.16
163. 1 Corinthians 14.1-5

164. 1 Corinthians 11.11, NIV.
165. 1 Corinthians 14.5
166. 1 Corinthians 14.26, NIV, 1984.
167. 1 Corinthians 14.31
168. 1 Timothy 2.11-12, NIV.
169. 1 Timothy 1.3 and 6
170. 1 Timothy 1.7
171. Acts 18.19-20
172. Acts 18.24-25
173. Acts 18.26
174. Acts 19.1-20
175. While I've seen blind eyes open, the deaf hear, and the lame walk, I've only witnessed an "extraordinary miracle" once. About six months ago, Kerry and I went to Ikea. We left the building fourteen minutes later — *and* we didn't buy anything.
176. Acts 19.9; see also 1 Corinthians 16.9
177. Acts 19.23
178. Acts 19.25
179. Acts 20.17; he did so shortly before Pentecost, vs.16, and had left Ephesus before the Passover, vs 6.
180. Acts 20.29
181. vs. 30
182. Acts 20.31
183. 1 Corinthians 1.25-29
184. Galatians 3.1
185. 1 Corinthians 15.32
186. 2 Timothy 4.14
187. 1 Timothy 1.3-4
188. 1 Timothy 4.7
189. 1 Timothy 5.6
190. 1 Timothy 5.13
191. 1 Timothy 5.14
192. See 1 Timothy 4.1
193. 1 Timothy 4.3
194. 1 Timothy 2.12, NIV.
195. KJV.
196. REB.
197. The Message.
198. 1 Corinthians 14.32-35, NIV.
199. 1 Corinthians 12.4-13
200. 1 Corinthians 14.28, 30 and 34; the same Greek word is used each time, *sigato*.

15
THE TWO SHALL BECOME ONE

Kerry and I have visited a number of churches of late. One is situated on a very attractive site, and has a most impressive building. The congregational mix of age and cultures is equally noteworthy, yet there were several things that made us feel uneasy. We'd already been in their bookstore and perused the offerings. What commanded attention there were the stacks and stacks of a particular systematic theology, a volume of heavy lifting that was definitely not for the faint of heart or spirit. And while waiting for the worship to begin, we had read their eighteen page Doctrinal Statement. It was handed to us at the welcome desk.

What we found most unsettling was the Connection Card in the little pockets in the sanctuary seating. It was no surprise that they wanted our personal details so that they knew that we were there. Nor was the space on the back of the card for our prayer requests, and a sentence assuring us that they'd be praying for us.

What signalled our concern was one of the tick boxes that featured on the front. Under the heading, My Marital Status, there were four options: Single, Married, Widowed, or Single Parent. For this church, the message was loud and clear — divorce is against the law.

However. But. Umm. While the vast majority of adults are married or partnered, the vast majority of relationships are considerably less than happy, healthy and fulfilling. It's been said that the modern definition of a family is a group of individuals gathered around a common flat screen, and you can tell when a family is breaking down. There's an increase in the number of flat screens it owns. While you're taking inventory, answer a quick survey question: do you know someone whom you would say has a great, mutually satisfying marriage? If you're married, is yours?

Just less than half of all marriages end in divorce. The UK Office of National Statistics puts the figure at forty-two per cent, Canadian StatsCan at forty-one per cent, and forty-five per cent in the US. An evangelical marriage is no guarantee for either happiness or longevity. In the UK, the Evangelical Alliance published their survey results in a paper titled "How's the Family?" They found that twenty-nine percent of respondents had sought help for relational difficulties; ten per cent had suffered physical abuse; and nine per cent had endured marital unfaithfulness. Roughly twenty-five per cent of the unions ended in divorce. These were Christian marriages.[201] This is a telling legacy. On many counts, the Church historically hasn't done a very good job at preparing people for marriage. It hasn't done a very good job nurturing couples in their marriages, or helping them in crises. And the Church hasn't done a very good job at bringing grace to bear in the midst of the pain and grief of a failed or failing marriage.

———•———

Before proceeding, the briefest of reviews is in order. Life is messy. We've all made a mess of at least some of it. No one of us gets it right, at least all of the time. We all fall short. The Good News in Jesus Christ is that God doesn't find fault with us, or our messes. He has no favourites[202] — we are all his beloved and accepted children, including those in failed and failing marriages. Jesus, "the Lamb of God who takes away the sin of the world,"[203] takes away all sin, including the complex of sins that precipitate divorce.

In Jesus Christ, God does not judge us according to our failings; rather, in Jesus he comes to seek and to save.[204] And God's mercy isn't just extended on the front end of conversion — we "who are being saved"[205] continue to have full access to grace, such that "if we confess our sins, he is just and may be trusted to forgive our sins and cleanse us from every kind of wrongdoing."[206] There's no fine-print that excludes the sin of divorce.

Presumably there's no disagreement with things so far. What unsettles so many in the church is that traditionally, the divorce texts in the New Testament are taken at face value. And a literal reading of those texts puts divorce, and the divorced, outside the realm of redeeming, restorative grace.

It's not just a biblical literalism that's the offender. Marriage is, by times, a tricky thing. And the human heart is a fragile organ. It's therefore understandable that we long for a sense of security, and a sense of stability in marriage. However, putting up a 'No Exit' sign over marriage simply doesn't solve all the traffic problems as two try to get to where they become one.

In the next five chapters, my hope is that a firm, graced foundation for marriage will be built — or rebuilt. And where things can't, or shouldn't be rebuilt, the question 'Where's grace in this?' will be applied to the pain and heart-break of divorce.

———•———

Let's start with the old story of the senior couple who celebrated fifty years of marriage. Their family and friends gathered for a big picnic, and it was a great day together. On the way home the

145

woman slowly, carefully said to her husband, "Herbert, you never tell me that you love me." He was dumbfounded. "Ethyl! I told you I loved you on our wedding day. If anything changes, you'll be the first to know."

Now the even older story, from the Creation account, and God's perfect plan and purpose for a man and a woman in marriage: "The two shall become one."[207] Herbert had it wrong. For fifty years, he misunderstood. He and Ethyl didn't mystically become one on their wedding day. The graced oneness that God purposes for their marriage was to be nurtured and grown, day by day, choice by choice. Herbert didn't do that, and that's why there was the unfulfilled longing in Ethyl's heart.

What it means for two to become one isn't spelled out explicitly in Scripture, either in the Creation story, or elsewhere. There actually isn't a great deal of detailed instruction on marriage in the Bible. We're going to have to piece things together, beginning with a foundational text found in the Book of Exodus. But note at the outset: it was addressed to a male-dominated culture that had both slaves and multiple wives. The situation was that a master — a man — had married his slave — a woman — but who now was going to marry a second wife. The passage reads: "If a man marries another woman, he must not deprive the first one of her food, clothing and marital rights."[208] The NIV is very polite there — in other translations the phrase "marital rights," is more explicitly translated, "conjugal rights."

Even this early into things, some of you may be thinking, 'This Old Testament text doesn't apply to us at all. We don't have multiple wives, and we don't marry slaves.' Agreed, but let's recognise the telling indictment that there are some spouses who currently feel like they're being treated like a slave.

Thousands of years ago, the Jewish Rabbis used this very

ancient text to establish timeless principles which apply to all marriages. Their thinking went like this: if a slave wife had the rights to food, clothing and conjugal rights, then a free wife would also certainly have the same rights. If one of two wives had those rights, then so did an only wife. And if a wife had these rights, then so did the husband.

Food, clothing, conjugal rights — or generically — nurture, care and intimacy — these are the foundational essentials of a godly, healthy, holy marriage. As these three essentials work their way deep into a relationship, 'two become one.' This text and the Rabbi's three principles are reflected in the Apostle Paul's teaching, as Eugene Peterson paraphrases: "The marriage bed must be a place of mutuality — the husband seeking to satisfy his wife, the wife seeking to satisfy her husband."[209] Unlike translations that speak of marital duty,[210] sexual rights,[211] or the completely obscure phrase, "render[ing] due benevolence,"[212] Peterson's paraphrase points to the shameless freedom and uninhibited intimacy that God purposes a husband and wife to share together, as underscored in the following verses: "The wife's body does not belong to her alone but also to her husband. In the same way, the husband's body does not belong to him alone but also to his wife. Do not deprive each other."[213]

The Apostle Paul wanted it clearly understood that a husband and wife are to freely give themselves to the other. The Apostle was no prude; mutual sexual enjoyment of one another is essential to a healthy, happy marriage. Add to this what Paul wrote in another letter: "Husbands, love your wives, just as Christ loved the church and gave himself up for her.... Husbands ought to love their wives as their own bodies. He who loves his wife loves himself. After all, no one ever hated their own body, but they feed and care for their own body."[214] Again, the giving of self, and the provision of food, clothing, conjugal love — nurture, care, intimacy — these foundational essentials are what define and grow a marriage — what it means for 'two becoming one.'

These essentials are reflected in the marriage vows. A thousand years ago, English brides promised that they would be 'bonny and buxom in bed and at board.' If you used a traditional wedding service, you may have promised conjugal love with these words: 'With my body I worship thee,' and nurture and care with the words 'I pledge thee my troth.' (Troth, not truck as spell-check insists.)

In contemporary services, a couple promises to 'love, honour and cherish' each other. But however it is worded, it's not the promise — the vow — that makes or breaks a marriage, because it's not speaking the words that make two become one. In the marriage ceremony, both sacred and civil, there is what's called the Consent. It is the fundamental, foundational basis of marriage. The question is asked, 'Do you, Billy Bob, take Betty Sue to be your lawfully wedded wife?' He answers, 'I do.' She does the same. Thereafter, it is the living out of the Consent which makes a marriage, the two becoming one.

Again, a bride and groom don't mystically become one on their wedding day. Billy Bob and Betty Sue grow into that graced oneness, day by day, choice by choice — by consent. Marriage formally begins on the wedding day, but marriage grows through a continuous, committed turning towards the other.

In a healthy, holy marriage, a husband and wife choose to turn towards the other regardless of their life's circumstances. They openly share their joys, their griefs, and their longings. They choose to open their hearts and spirits to each other. They choose to continuously give themselves to the other. Listening, kindness, affection, romance — these are all expressions of the giving of self to the other. They are the expression of nurture, care, and intimacy. It is this continuous turning towards each other that grows a greater, fuller oneness.

The opposite is a withholding. For fifty years, Herbert withheld nurture from Ethyl. On his wedding day, he said, 'I do,' but he didn't. He withheld those simple, tender words, 'I love you.' At any point, at any moment, a husband or wife can choose to turn away from the other. They can choose to shut the other out. In fact, the word 'divorce' in Hebrew comes from the root word that means to 'cut off.' Lest the severity of turning away be lost in translation, the same Hebrew word is used for both amputation[215] and decapitation.[216] Shutting the other out always has serious consequences for a marriage.

Back to the wedding ceremony. Consent means that a husband and wife commit themselves to turning towards each other, to extend to the other a lifetime of nurture, care, and intimacy. For instance, in terms of love and respect, try answering these questions about yourself and your spouse, or yourself and your partner. If you're single, think of how you remember your father and mother's relationship. *My spouse is interested in my opinion. My spouse cares about what I'm feeling. We often touch each other. When we disagree, we're willing to listen to each other. We respect each other's ideas and feelings. We are genuinely good friends. We are affectionate toward each other. My partner takes good care of me.*

If you answer Yes to those questions, you have just traced a committed turning towards the other. If you answer No, that more than likely signals a habitual turning away from the other, the evidence of defective consent.

And that's what breaks a marriage — defective consent — when there is stubborn, habitual unfaithfulness to the covenantal promises made on the wedding day. When there is stubborn, habitual refusal to turn towards the other, when one or both 'cut the other off' rather than draw themselves close, spouses choose *not* to give themselves to the other. They choose to deprive the other of the nurture, care, and intimacy that's required for 'two to become one.'

Think of it this way. When Billy Bob met Betty Sue, there was an initial attraction. 'Oooh!' 'Ummm!' It's like each of them grabs an end of a four foot long piece of theraband, the stretchy rubber exercise tubing that physiotherapists use. There's something there that draws Billy Bob and Betty Sue together. As they courted, they drew closer together. They thoroughly enjoyed turning towards each other.

They got married, but a couple of years in, she lost the grace for her job. She battled every morning as she got herself ready, and dragged herself home at night. He lost his job and couldn't find a new one. The money was tight. They each had some health issues, and a bit of family drama ensued with her parents. All in, it was a stressful situation, for months and months and months.

Betty Sue could have started nagging, and criticising, and finding fault with Billy Bob. He could have become sarcastic, taken his frustrations out on her, and withdrawn deep into his man-cave. If any of that had happened, it would be like the two of them pulling away from each other — increasing the tension on the stretchy theraband.

She could have started watching the entire box set of *Sex and the City*, and he, endless re-runs of *Top Gear* — on their own flat screens. They could have deprived each other sexually, adding further tension and strain to the relationship, and creating even greater distance between them.

Alternatively, in the same exact circumstances, they could have continuously chosen to turn towards the other. When she was having an especially hard morning she could say, 'I think I've lost my peace somewhere.' He could have wrapped his arms around her and prayed blessing over her. Instead of losing themselves in front of the tv, they could have opened a bottle of wine, cuddled on the sofa, and talked... or just held each other. They could have given themselves to the other sexually, even though they didn't initially feel like it, knowing that intimacy was a graced glue that would help hold them together.

———·———

As it stands, I've painted an either/or scenario — either turning towards, or turning from. But just as there are no perfect people, there are no perfect marriage partners, and no perfect marriages. My apologies if that comes as a shock.

The psychologist John Gottman has made the study of marriage his life's work. He has an excellent book: *Why Marriages Succeed or Fail*. Though he doesn't use these particular words, he says that for a marriage to be healthy, the essentials of nurture, care and intimacy have to be expressed more often than criticism, defensiveness and withdrawal. There needs to be considerably more turning towards than there is turning away. He has a working ratio for what he calls successful marriages. It's quite telling if it seems excessive to you. Gottman's ratio is five to one. Choosing to turn towards the other five times as much as turning away! Five kind, generous, nurturing, loving acts for every screw-up.

Maybe you think that's too contrived. Maybe you feel that it's completely unreasonable, or unnecessary to even consider keeping track of things like that. The thing is, if you don't intentionally choose to work at repairing and rebuilding things relationally when you've blown it, things will bankrupt. There are no tricks here. If your investments don't exceed your withdrawals, your upkeep will be your downfall.

Notes

201. http://eauk.org/snapshot/upload/EA-FAMILY-REPORT-WEB-2.pdf

202. Acts 10.34

203. John 1.29

204. John 3.16-17; Luke 19.10

205. Acts 2.47 NIV.

206. 1 John 1.9

207. Genesis 2.24

208. Exodus 21.10; see REB, NASB. NLT is even more explicit, translating the phrase as "sexual intimacy."

209. 1 Corinthians 7.3, *The Message*.

210. NIV.

211. NET.

212. KJV.

213. 1 Corinthians 7.3-5, NIV, 1984.

214. Ephesians 5.25, 28-9, NIV. Paul's statement, "no one hates his own body" clearly implies he'd never been to Junior High school.

215. Leviticus 22.24

216. 1 Samuel 17.51

16

WHAT MAKES AND BREAKS A MARRIAGE

———•———

If you're ever stuck for a wedding present, give the happy couple a toaster. A decent toaster should last ten years. Pray that their marriage lasts that long.

In the previous chapter, some of the consequences of turning away from the other were mapped. I quoted John Gottman's five-to-one ratio for successful marriages. In what follows, I hope to make explicit what it takes to grow a marriage, what turning towards the other looks like. Without being prescriptive, I hope to describe how to soften a hard heart, how to warm a cold heart, how to enliven a dead heart. And not just one's own. What follows has the power to restore one's partner.

It's a question of investments. Not financial, but relational investments.[217] Especially in marriage, each and every one of us works out of a relational bank account. Day in, day out, week in, week out, we make deposits and withdrawals.

Every time we listen attentively, when we honour and respect the other, when we're generous, kind, honest, patient, and thoughtful, we make deposits in our relational bank. When we give of ourselves; when we share our hopes and dreams, our fears and worries; when we open ourselves to the other; when we seek to please the other, the relationship gets richer. The quality of our being together gets better, stronger, fuller. We know more of the glorious oneness that God purposes for a husband and wife.

And every time we're dirty dogs, every time we're only interested in what we get out of the relationship; when we're only there when it's convenient; when we're stingy with our time; when we're indifferent and uncaring; when we're rude, rough, disrespectful, dishonest; when we nurture grudges, and make a big deal of past hurts and disappointments; when we insist that the other meets our needs, we make significant withdrawals from the account. The quality of our being together diminishes and degenerates. That's what happens when we take, rather than give.

When we do our own thing, when we become self-absorbed, be it with work, with golf or with the kids... when anything else has the balance of our attention, and interest, and energy, there's a drain on the relationship. The trend lines will be heading in the wrong direction. There's a very simple reason: there is a consistent devaluation of our relational stock.

Whether we're aware of it or not, we're always working against a bottom line. In a bull run, that's no worry. When we were courting and we were smitten with each other, the relationship was full, flush, if you will. Presumably, there was a healthy bank balance. Investor confidence was high, and dividends were lavish. We were having a wonderful time with each other, and life was grand. That's why we got married — we hoped that things would just keep getting better and better, richer and richer.

But happy couples only ride off into the sunset and live happily ever-after in fairy tales. Sooner or later, we live with disappointment and disillusionment. Our knight in shining armour needs polishing, and our Fair Lady isn't quite. And most of us have to contend with distraction and the often contradictory tensions generated by work and the kids. Things with our spouse begin to turn thin relationally, and we start spending more than we invest. When things get grim and stay that way, the marriage is in recession. Over the long haul there can come a time when withdrawals exceed deposits, and things are completely collapsed. There comes a day when relational bankruptcy has to be declared.

Marriage, like most of life, is no get-rich-quick scheme. The vows we make to one another on our wedding day are declarations of our intentions to make long-term deposits that pay big dividends. Living out those vows has us making deposits that are blue-chip investments, such that our spouse is truly our life-partner, and our friends will celebrate our fiftieth anniversary with us.

There are two investment keys to a relational portfolio. The first is honour. Honour has to do with respect, with esteem. It's sending the message continuously, 'Who you are, our friendship, our relationship, our being together — it means the world to me.' To honour each other means continuously sending the message that you count the other special, and you want them to know it.

Honour is shown in the little things, and it works like compounding interest on your investments. Honour is something beyond basic consideration of the other. It is creative. Honour looks for ways to bless. To build. To encourage. It is doing something extra, because you care. For instance, Kerry and I share an electric toothbrush. She has a little red ring on her brush head. Mine is blue. When we're done brushing, we change the heads for the other, because it's one small way to say, 'I'm glad I get to share life with you.' Honour means sending Kerry a random text reminding her, just in case she got distracted, that I love her. It means making Thai curries that are so hot they make my nose run, because that's the way she likes them.

So far so good. Now it's time to scratch the underbelly. The second investment key is the commitment to take responsibility for withdrawals. To apologise. To ask forgiveness. Consider the following: 'I'm sorry. I was way out of line. Can we start again?'

Virtually all of us are physically capable of saying those words. It's a function of will. The issue is whether or not we choose to. It takes a great deal of character to seek reconciliation, to ask for, and to extend forgiveness. By times, it's desperately difficult. By times it requires facing conflict head-on. By times it means dealing with long-standing problems, perhaps deep within, or in the relationship. Often it's both. But these acts of courage pay big dividends because forgiveness cancels our relational debts. If we won't say 'I'm sorry, please forgive me,' we're draining one of our relationship's biggest equity pools.

If there is a habitual dishonouring of the other, and if there is a habitual refusal to reconcile and repair the relationship, things will bankrupt.

———·———

The financial markets preoccupy the daily news week in, week out. It's all very immediate, with but superficial analysis, lots of speculation, and gloomy prognosticating. Have you read any good news about the markets this month?

There's essentially nothing any of us can do about the future of our financial investments. There's nothing any of us can do about the financial institutions that are in such dire straits, except despair. (I suppose panic is another option.)

Over our relational portfolio, we each have considerable influence. One of the usual phrases that is used in a wedding ceremony is 'for better or worse.' Regardless of circumstance, we determine the deposits and the withdrawals that either make or break our marriage. We choose to honour the other, and we choose to forgive. We choose to give of ourselves and share, just as we choose to turn away and withhold. It's a choice, and there's nothing to keep us from growing our relationship such that we're stupidly wealthy, because the key to relational wealth is very simple: make regular, generous deposits, and take early responsibility for your withdrawals. Put in more than you take out.

———•———

I appreciate that for some readers, this whole analogy doesn't work. It's too calculated, too forced, too unromantic. I understand. But talk to someone who's been in serious financial debt. They got that way for one, simple reason: spending exceeded earnings. They faced bankruptcy because withdrawals exceeded deposits. Turning that around was hard, very hard intentional work. They had to be very calculating in the way they dug themselves out. They will be quick to say that there was nothing romantic about it. But it changed their life.

Talk to someone who has faced serious relational debt. They got that way for the same, simple reason: spending exceeded earnings. They faced bankruptcy because withdrawals exceeded deposits. Turning that around was hard, very hard intentional work. They had to be very calculating in the way they dug themselves out. They will be quick to say that there was nothing romantic about it. But it changed their life, and it redeemed their relationship.

———•———

One of the most quoted wedding readings comes from a passage where the Apostle Paul wrote, not specifically of married love, but generally of the love which allows another to grow and come to fulfilment. It fits in a wedding because it's especially true of the love required to enrich a marriage.

Love is patient and kind. Love envies no one, is never boastful, is never conceited, never rude; love is never selfish, never quick to take offence. Love keeps no score of wrongs, takes no pleasure in the sins of others, but delights in the truth. There is nothing love cannot face; there is no limit to its faith, its hope, its endurance. Love will never come to an end.[218]

This is a description of perfect love, and the best love can be. Love that is always patient, always kind. Love that is never rude, never angry. Love that knows no limits, no end; love that is never failing.

This is where grace does its work. If we choose to be patient, if we commit to kindness, if we find ways to honour, these expressions of love liberate something in us, and may do something the same in our spouse. These expressions of love restore something in us, and may heal something in our relationship. These expressions of love re-kindle something in our own hearts, and may stir something in our spouse or partner. The American poet WH Auden understood relational banking. He put it this way: "If equal affection cannot be/let the more loving one be me."[219]

If you're married, you might want to put this book down, go find your spouse, and reach out and take them by the hand. Look him in the eye, look her in the eye. Smile. Try to remember something of the affection you felt back when you were courting. Then ask, 'Could we start again?'

Notes
217. The illustration is taken from Steven Covey, *Seven Habits of Highly Effective People*, Fireside: New York, 1989, p.188.
218. 1 Corinthians 13.4-8
219. "The More Loving One", lines 7-8.

17

NO LIFETIME GUARANTEE

——•——

When I was fifteen years old, Jack Serez showed up at our front door one evening. He was asking for me. Jack lived two doors down from us, and initially I thought I was in trouble for something I'd done in the neighbourhood.

He hadn't come to rat me out to my parents. Jack owned a small carpentry company that specialised in kitchen and bathroom renovations. He asked, "Would you be interested in wrecking on Saturdays?" "Wrecking??" I didn't know what it involved, but it sounded like it would be a blast. Jack explained. "I'll take you to the job site, and you'll strip the kitchen cabinets from the wall, rip off the old ceramic tile, sometimes the plaster, sometimes the flooring. It's hard, dirty work, but a workman is worth his labour."

The next Saturday, I went to work wrecking. All through high school, and nine years of university, I worked for Jack. The first few jobs were pure, unleashed testosterone. I'd smash away with a twelve-pound sledge hammer, reducing everything to smithereens. When I showered at the end of the day, I'd be too tired to lift my arms to wash my hair. (I had hair back then.)

Months later, over lunch-time, I overheard one of Jack's other employees mumble, *"Strong like bull, smart like streetcar."* I knew he was talking about me. He'd grown tired of watching me mindlessly obliterate everything around me. I decided then that I'd learn how things came apart — how to 'de'-construct — rather than just bull and tear. So, I learned my carpentry backwards. In learning how things came apart, I learned how to put them together.

That meant I needed to buy some tools. One of my first purchases was a twenty-two ounce framing hammer. I still have it. I bought that hammer soon after I started working for Jack, so, we've been together for over forty years.

My hammer is exquisitely designed to pound things all day long, week after week, month after month. For over forty years, I've pounded nails with it. I've whacked studs into place. I've ripped stuff up with it. I've dropped it off roofs, I've dropped it off ladders, I've smashed concrete with it. For over forty years, I have unapologetically abused it. But that's what it was designed for. So much so, that it comes with a lifetime guarantee. If it doesn't stand up to continuous, habitual, pounding abuse, if it fails in any way, the manufacturers will replace it — no exceptions, no questions asked.

———•———

Like the 'No divorce' church introduced in the previous chapter, there are those that think God designed marriage just the same way. Regardless of habitual, pounding abuse — regardless of the failure — a lifetime guarantee is in place, the 'till death doth us part' that the Church built into the traditional wedding vows. But a human heart is not a hammer. A framing hammer is designed to take a lifetime of pounding; a human heart is not. Nor is marriage as God intends it to be.

What follows builds on the previous chapters. In the Creation story, we have the defining statement of God's ideal for marriage: "A man leaves his father and mother and attaches himself to his wife, and the two become one."[220] The two become one as a husband and a wife give of themselves, to and for the other. Theirs is a promised, covenanted exclusivity. One man, one woman. And so the wedding vow, 'With you and no other.'

From Exodus 21.10, nurture, care and intimacy are the foundational essentials that determine a godly, healthy, holy marriage, what it means for "two becoming one." That oneness grows over time as a couple continuously turn towards each other. Should they choose to turn away, there are serious consequences. Think of the theraband illustration again. If there is a big turning away, if the relationship is strained and stretched far enough, for long enough, something is going to snap, and you can be sure that it's going to hurt. There is a relational breaking point. That's why there are biblical admonitions against adultery; being with another lover tears to pieces the marital oneness. The adulterer is unfaithful to the covenant promise of exclusivity he or she made to their spouse. They haven't just turned away; they've let go and gone after another.

The covenant of marital faithfulness is an image of the loving commitment that God hopes his people will promise him — and will then live out. He hopes that his people will ever turn towards him, as he turns towards them. Generation after generation, it hasn't work out well. In the Old Testament book of Hosea for instance, there is a running parallel between the prophet Hosea's marriage to Gomer, and God's marriage to the people of Israel. Gomer was a harlot, and was unfaithful to her husband Hosea, not just once or twice, but habitually. So too, Israel was adulterous and unfaithful, turning away to worship other gods. And things snapped. Just as Hosea divorced Gomer for her unfaithfulness, so God said of Israel, "She is no longer my wife, nor am I her husband."[221]

In the book of Ezekiel, it's even more explicit. God said to Israel,

"I gave you my solemn oath and entered into a covenant with you — and you became mine."[222] God nurtured Israel, cared for her, and gave himself to her, the same three principles of covenant faithfulness in marriage that are named in Exodus 21. Sadly, in Ezekiel's day, Israel didn't reciprocate; she prostituted herself time and again such that God exclaimed, "You adulterous wife! You prefer strangers to your own husband!"[223] Similar conduct was indicted in the book of Isaiah, and the question was asked, "Where is your mother's certificate of divorce with which I sent her away?"[224] Because of Israel's habitual unfaithfulness, God divorced her.

———•———

But back to the marriage between a man and a woman. When a bride and groom stare dreamily into each other's eyes and say their 'I do's, they don't mystically become one on their wedding day. The two become one. They *grow* into a graced oneness, day by day, choice by choice. To that end, the Creation story talks about 'leaving and cleaving' — leaving father and mother, and cleaving, becoming united with their spouse.[225]

That's the wonderful, glorious ideal. The reality is that we each come from a family of origin, for better or worse. Among other things, our caregivers establish for us our understanding and experience of security, identity, and belonging — again, for better or worse. But none of us had perfect parents, and there are no perfect homes. That means we all have issues around security, identity, and belonging.

Say, for instance, that our man Billy Bob grew up in a family that never apologised to one another. They'd yell, and call each other names, and slam doors, and then the next morning behave as if nothing had happened. No attempts were made at resolution, and no reconciliation was sought. Not only was it a very dysfunctional way of dealing with conflict; it also had distorting consequences in terms of Billy Bob's sense of security, and identity, and belonging.

He gets married. As God designed things, Billy Bob is to leave and to cleave to his wife, Betty Sue. Part of emotional maturity is independence. If Billy Bob is still emotionally dependent on his family of origin, he'll continue to rant and rave, yell and slam doors, just like his parents and siblings. He hasn't matured to the place where he recognises that this is not a healthy way of dealing with conflict. He doesn't realise the damaging erosion that is taking place in his bride's sense of security, identity and belonging.

If, instead, there's an emotional independence, Billy Bob and his Betty Sue have the opportunity to create a new family system, and a new way of relating to each other. For theirs to be a healthy, holy marriage, Billy Bob has to leave his family's dysfunctional way of dealing with conflict. When he's upset, he is going to have to learn to say something along the lines of: 'Honey, we have a problem. Can we talk about it?' When he messes up, he needs to learn to say something like, 'Babe, I was way out of line. Please forgive me. I am so sorry.'

That's some of what it means to cleave to Betty Sue. Choosing to apologise to his wife, to talk through their differences, to turn towards her in the midst of conflict — all of that demonstrates a healthy independence from his family of origin's unhealthy influence. She'll need to be doing the same.

While all of this is essential, too much independence can cost a marriage. Too much independence will compromise the cleaving as the two become one. Typically, it's signalled around control issues. If you've been in a relationship for longer than about fifteen minutes, you've probably noticed that the person you're trying to relate to isn't a clone. They don't think exactly like you do. They don't react to things exactly like you do. They don't feel things, see things, hear things exactly like you do. John Grey made a fortune playing this single string in his book, *Men are from Mars, Women from Venus*. If either or both spouses stubbornly insist that the other do things their way, the oneness of their marriage will be compromised.

If it always has to be my way, there'll be trouble. When I lived alone, when I was independent, the toilet seat was usually up. I squeezed the toothpaste from the bottom of the tube till it was empty, and I would often do my dishes when there wasn't any counter space left.

There is no universal, categorical, non-negotiable position for toilet seats, or strategies for squeezing toothpaste and washing up dishes. My way was what worked for me. That's how *I* did it. In marriage, for two to become one, it means that I choose to shift from an independent *I and my* to *We and our*. If, in the middle of the night, I hear a little scream from the bathroom, I need to apologise for leaving the toilet seat up, for doing things my way.

Again, by way of review, there is the biblical counsel, "Husbands, love your wives, just as Christ loved the church and gave himself up for her."[226] Husbands and wives are to give themselves to each other, including conjugal rights, and ought not to "deprive each other."[227] This, because a husband is to please his wife, and a wife is to please her husband.[228] Paul was trained as a Rabbinic scholar, and in both these texts he was echoing Exodus 21.10 and the marital promises of food, clothing, and conjugal intimacy.

Now, a no-brainer: no one divorces when they are happily married, when there's a mutual, committed turning towards the other. But for the "hardness of heart,"[229] when there is continuous turning away from the other, the pain and the grief can create such a toxic environment that home-life is unsustainable. If there is a turning away that habitually indulges pornography, or unfaithfulness that ends in adultery; a turning away that is chronic neglect, let alone abuse; a turning away that is relational or emotional abandonment, there's no union, there's no oneness, and the marriage is functionally dead.

The Apostle Paul said in such circumstances, one is not bound to a deserting spouse.[230] Literally, the New Testament Greek word is stronger than "bound" — it's "enslaved." Where there is habitual, continuous turning away from the other, one is no longer enslaved to that marriage, because of the hardness of heart.

Back to where we started. My hammer is designed to take a lifetime of pounding. I don't think twice about picking it up and abusing it. The manufacturer expects me to smash, and bash and demolish things with it. The manufacturer guarantees that it will take a lifetime of — well — suffering. In contrast, the human heart is a fragile thing. In marriage, the heart is to be cared for. The heart is to be nurtured.

Some of you, dear readers, are in loveless, care-less marriages. Some of you suffer chronic neglect. Some of you are habitually abused, emotionally, relationally, physically. There haven't been any signs of a commitment to cleave, a turning towards, for a very, very long time. Any emotional or physical intimacy is a distant memory.

That's not how God designed marriage. That's not how God designed spouses to treat each other. There is grace, right now, for those who are willing to repent — to turn — to turn towards their spouse, and start again. There is grace, right now, for those who are willing to habitually turn towards their partner. To commit, again, to exclusivity. To commit, again, to nurture. To commit, again, to pleasing and satisfying the other. To commit to leaving the old, and cleaving to the new.

But where the heart is hard, where the heart is stubborn, where there is habitual refusal of the other, the covenant of marriage has been grossly breached. There is defective consent. Instead of 'I do,' there is a chronic 'I don't, and I won't.' Hammers come with a lifetime guarantee. Marriages do not.

Notes
220. Genesis 2.24
221. Hosea 2.2
222. Ezekiel 16.18b, NIV.
223. Ezekiel 16.32, NIV.
224. Isaiah 50.1, NIV.
225. See Genesis 2.24
226. Ephesians 5.25, NIV.
227. 1 Corinthians 7.3 and 5, NIV.
228. Verses 33 and 35
229. Matthew 19.8, NASB.
230. 1 Corinthians 7.15: *dedoulotai.*

18

THOSE WHOM GOD HAS JOINED

———•———

Early in the Creation story God said, "Let us make human beings in our image, after our likeness."[231] In understanding this text, the Russian Orthodox theologians make an all-important distinction between image and likeness. Every single human being is made in the image of God, even the most barbaric, the most inhuman. The trouble is, they don't bear any likeness.

The image denotes our potentiality for life in God; the likeness, our realisation of that potentiality. That's where we all live out life, in between image and likeness, potential and realisation. And the Apostle Paul declared the ultimate standard: "If I have no love, I am nothing."[232] If we are unloving, we still bear the image of God, but have no likeness, because God is love. We haven't lived up to our potential.

A loveless marriage bears the image of what God intends, but has no likeness. A husband and wife have not realised their marriage potential.

———•———

Let's return yet again to the Creation account. Woman was created from man, for man. From one came two, and in marriage the two become one. That oneness was created as Adam and Eve gave of themselves, to and for the other. And both of them were having a great time doing so: "Adam and his wife were both naked, and they felt no shame."[233] Which is another way of repeating the way the creation account in Genesis 1 concludes: "It was very good."[234]

But not for long. Genesis 3 tells the story of the temptation and the Fall, and an ominous note is sounded: "The eyes of both of them were opened, and they knew that they were naked."[235] Previously, Adam and Eve gloriously and intimately enjoyed one another and their unique differences. Now, with eyes open, there is a dishonouring of the differentiation. Now, they're finding fault with each other: 'Hey Eve, What's wrong with you? Why aren't you like me?' And it's not just the fault-finding. The two whom God intended to rule as one now attempt to rule each other.

One ruling over another never goes well, and so there is in the Old Testament the recognition that marriage can get so bad that if a man finds in his wife "something offensive," when she "finds no favour in his eyes," when there's "something wrong with her," then he can divorce her.[236] A union can degenerate such that it suffers distortion, domination, even destruction.

Now a big jump to Jesus, and with Jesus, his message: "Repent, for the Kingdom of Heaven is upon you."[237] We are invited to change the way we think, and change the way we see things, because the Kingdom is creation healed. Whatever a person's brokenness, their soul-sickness, their sin, when they meet Jesus, he brings merciful restoration. That's the Gospel, the Good News.

With that in hand, we head to what Jesus taught on marriage. But note this: what follows doesn't come from a First Century marriage enrichment weekend. It comes in a time of opposition. The religious of the day, the Pharisees, were on the offensive. They asked Jesus what sounds like a straightforward question, but it was far from being a genuine one. They asked: "Is it lawful for a man to divorce his wife for any and every reason?"[238]

Traditionally, that question has sent interpreters down all manner of rabbit trails. What does divorce "for any and every reason" mean? Some have had job security theologising about that phrase, and the similar divorce phrases in Deuteronomy 24 — when a wife does "something offensive" and "becomes unpleasing." What is allowed? Where does the line get drawn? When is enough enough?

The thing is, the Pharisees weren't asking theological questions about divorce. They weren't even legitimate questions in their own right. That might come as a shock, so let me buy a bit of time. What are the three most important factors for property values? Location, location, location. It's the same with Bible interpretation: Location, location, location. Or better: Context, context, context.

Here in Matthew 19, the passage doesn't begin with the Pharisee's question about divorce, but with these words: "[Jesus] left Galilee and came into the region of Judea on the other side of the Jordan."[239] Judea... the Jordan.... Does that bring anybody to mind? How about John the Baptist? In terms of location, this is not a safe neighbourhood in which to be answering questions about divorce. Herod of Judea had John the Baptist imprisoned and subsequently beheaded him.[240] Why? Because John had looked Herod straight in the eye and told him: "It is not lawful for you to have [your brother's wife.]"[241] (The backstory runs like this: Herod became smitten with Herodias, who was married to Herod's brother Philip. Herod divorced his first wife, Herodias left Philip, and they got married.)

Back to Matthew 19.3. The Pharisees came to Jesus, but not with a genuine theological question about divorce. They came "to test him." The word translated here as "test" is the same word used when Jesus was led into the wilderness, and "tempted" by the devil.[242] The Pharisees hoped to trap Jesus. They hoped to destroy him, just like the devil hoped to destroy Jesus. And they used — misused — Scripture, just like the devil did.

The Pharisees asked Jesus, "Is it lawful...?" Hear the echo in the question? John had told Herod, "It is not lawful," and it got him beheaded. The Pharisees were hoping that with any luck, Jesus would give the same answer. Then they could relay that to Herod, and he'd have Jesus beheaded.

They were not asking a theological question, but a political one. The Pharisees had been meeting with Herod's men repeatedly. Together, they plotted "how they could assassinate Jesus."[243] Earlier, the Pharisees and Herod's men had tried to trap Jesus with their question about paying taxes.[244] The scheme went like this: nobody likes paying taxes, especially when they're oppressively high. If Jesus took the side of the poor and absolved them of their civil duty, then the Pharisees and Herod's men could accuse him of insurrection, and he would be executed as a traitor. But if he upheld Rome's right to taxation, he was no friend of the masses. But Jesus "saw through their duplicity."[245]

Back again to Matthew 19. The Pharisees knew the Law inside and out, upside and downside. That was their job. They knew Deuteronomy 24.1, the text that clearly states that divorce was lawful. There's no question. It's in the Book. And they knew Leviticus 18.16, the "Thou shalt not" that prohibits a man having sexual relations with his brother's wife. That was presumably the text that John quoted to Herod, and it's what got his head cut off. The Pharisees just hoped that Jesus would answer the same way, and that when they told Herod how Jesus felt about his marriage to Herodias, Herod would react to Jesus like he did to John, and there would be another beheading.

Jesus knew it was a set-up, and asked his own question. In effect it went like this: 'Before the Law — back to the beginning, to Genesis, how was it then? Before the distortion and the destruction? "The two, become one." That's what God purposes in marriage.' Then he added a new, relational component, something that was not in the Law: "What God has joined together, man must not separate."[246]

This is Kingdom marriage. Marriage that is healing, and restoring, and redeeming. "What God has joined." There is a graced giving of self to the other. In the present discussion with the Pharisees, there's implicit contrast, because Herod took his brother's wife. It was lust that joined them, not God. Theirs was something far less than a Kingdom marriage, a graced union.

The Pharisees didn't give up easily, so they pressed Jesus with Deuteronomy 24: "Why then did Moses command that a man give his wife a certificate of divorce and send her away?" Maybe they could get Jesus to blaspheme against Moses and the Law. They'd have to do their own dirty work then, but they were required to stone blasphemers …. That'd work….

Jesus did it to them again: "Moses permitted you to divorce your wives because your hearts were hard."[247] (Notice the shift — the Pharisees spoke of "commanding" divorce, and Jesus used the word "permit.") As Jesus teaches, divorce is a provisional mercy extended because of the stubbornness, or the hardness, of heart. Divorce isn't required; it's allowed, because marriage can be so toxic, so destructive, so distorted that two people can't keep living that way. But that's not what God intends.

And then, Jesus pulled a fast one with the Pharisees: "If a man" — imagine that he nods in the direction of Herod's palace — "divorces his wife for any cause other than unchastity in order to marry another, he commits adultery,"[248] so, if there's going to be any stoning, take that back to Herod, the adulterer, and read Deuteronomy 22.22 to him and explain to him why it is you have to stone both him and Herodias — to "purge Israel of this wickedness."

———•———

In the following verses, the disciples totally misunderstood what's been at stake. So has most of the Church thereafter. Some of you are thinking, 'Hang on, Matthew 19.9 in my Bible reads "if a man divorces his wife *and* marries another, ... he commits adultery." *And*, not '*in order to*.' I know. The New Testament Greek word in question is *kai*. It's a connecting, joining word. A copulative, if you know your grammar. We get the word 'couple' from the same root. It's a fluid word that has more than one meaning, and is translated in several different ways, depending on the context: "and, but, also, indeed, even, so then, if, therefore, when, yet, in order to."[249]

Here in Matthew 19, Jesus didn't make a general, across the board statement about divorce. He sprung the trap that the Pharisees had laid for him. It's not just anybody's divorce that was in question — it was Herod's. He divorced in order to marry another. And Jesus said, that's the equivalent of adultery.[250]

———•———

I appreciate that some of you may be working on yet another fur ball. Let's back up to square one, and all agree that divorce, any divorce, every divorce is a grievous departure from God's will for our marriages. Yes? But we're all living a grievous departure from God's will — for our lives. Yes? That's why we all need a Saviour. Yes?

In Jesus, there is Kingdom mercy, forgiveness of sin, new life, healing, restoration, and redemption, because "the Kingdom of heaven is at hand." All that's required is the recognition that we need it. That we're a failure. That we've made a mess of things. And not just before we got saved. We need grace every single day. Every single minute of every single day. We continue to make mistakes. We continue to mess up. We continue to make bad choices. In technical theological terms, we are being sanctified. We, and our marriages, are works in progress.

If we insist that everything is hunky-dory, that we're managing just fine, thank you; if we insist that we're a success, then there's no hope for us, because Jesus only forgives sinners. If, for instance, you're proud of your marital fidelity, be very careful in passing judgment on those whose marriages have failed. Because Jesus made it very clear that if you've looked on a woman with a lustful eye, you've wanted to take that which is not yours.[251] Remember, oneness in marriage comes as two give of themselves to and for the other. When you take that which is not yours, you've committed adultery in your heart. You've been unfaithful in your heart, and that has profound consequences for the marriage you're so very proud of.

There is not a man alive who has not desired a woman other than his wife, and been critical of his wife for not being more like the one he desires. Probably not a woman either. We've all missed the mark. We are all below the line. We all, each and every one of us, need mercy. (Now would be a good time to say, 'Amen.')

The traditional, rigid interpretation of the divorce passages essentially means that unmerited, undeserved, unconditional Kingdom mercy does not extend to those whose marriages have failed. Consequently, divorce may not be the unforgivable sin, but that interpretation makes it the unredeemable one. Where's grace in that?

The traditional, rigid interpretation of the divorce passages also fails to ask Kingdom questions that require discernment: Was it a marriage that God brought together? Were there miracles of grace that evidenced the Kingdom's power and presence? Were there signs of God's blessing? Or, instead of two giving themselves to each other, was it more of a taking relationship, where each looked to the other to meet their own needs? Was it lust-driven, and so, something far less than a Kingdom union? Without redeeming grace at work on an ongoing basis, every relationship is bound to suffer distortion and grief, the consequences of hardness of heart, and unsoftened stubbornness.

———•———

There's a most remarkable declaration buried in the middle of the little book of Jonah. In the space of thirteen words, it explains the whole of human history, our own personal histories, and why it is marriages fail. Ready? "Those who cling to worthless idols forfeit the grace that could be theirs."[252]

An idol, what we worship, is that which gives us 'security.' An idol is that which gives us 'significance,' that which gives us 'satisfaction.' There are some marriages that fail because commitment to the workplace takes precedence over the relationship. Work has been idolised. There's the mistaken belief that work gives more security, significance and satisfaction than becoming one with the beloved. Some marriages fail because of adultery — the new lover is looked to for security, significance, and satisfaction. It is also possible to idolise a victim mentality. That's why the words security, significance and satisfaction are all in inverted commas, because if we cling to a defective self-understanding, or shame, or unforgiveness; if we cling to fear, or unredeemed woundings — or a toxic cocktail of the lot — we forfeit the grace that could be ours.

Recall the elastic theraband illustration. If one or both partners cling to an idol, they've let go of that which draws them together. If their commitment to clinging is greater than their commitment to turning towards the other they are, in fact, turning away. And doing so, they cut themselves off from the healing, redeeming, restorative grace that Jesus wants to work into their lives and their marriages, the grace that makes all things new. That turning away means they forfeit the graced likeness — the life of redeeming love — that God purposes for their lives and marriages. They have failed to realise their potential.

Notes

231. Genesis 1.26
232. 1 Corinthians 13.2
233. Genesis 2.25, NIV.
234. Genesis 1.31
235. Genesis 3.7
236. Deuteronomy 24.1, REB, KJV, NLT.
237. Matthew 4.17
238. Matthew 19.3, NIV.
239. Matthew 19.1
240. Matthew 14.3-10
241. See Matthew 14.4
242. Matthew 4.1
243. Mark 3.6, NET.
244. Mark 12.13-17
245. Mark 12.15
246. See Matthew 19.4-6
247. Matthew 19.8, NIV.
248. See Matthew 19.9
249. Liddell and Scott, *Greek-English Lexicon*. New York: Harper and Brothers, 1883, p.726.
250. David Intone-Brewer, *Divorce and Remarriage*, Eerdmans, 2002, p.161.
251. See Mathew 5.27-28
252. Jonah 2.8, NIV, 1984.

19
FOR ANY REASON

—·—

Consider the following straightforward statement: *"Sixteen year olds should be allowed to drink."* How does that sound to you? Would you vote YES on a referendum?

Very few of those over sixteen tick the YES box. But if those sixteen and under aren't allowed to drink, they'll dehydrate, and eventually die. (I know, some of you are thinking: 'And that's a problem?')

You presumed that I was asking, 'Should sixteen year olds be allowed to drink *alcohol*.' I didn't make any mention of it at all, but you knew that was implied, that it was the context for my question. Youth Services can hold public awareness meetings on Under-age Drinking; teens are issued ASBOs for under-age drinking; if someone looks rough and ragged on a Saturday morning you conclude, 'They had too much to drink Friday night.' Absolutely no mention of alcohol is made in any of those situations, yet we know that booze is the subject of the matter at hand.

"If a sixteen year old drinks, he is breaking the law." Implied in that straightforward statement is, "If a sixteen year old drinks *alcohol*, he is breaking the law." And there's no need to make explicit, to detail, what a sixteen year old can legally drink: water, coke, juice. We all know that. It goes without saying. Right? It

goes without saying.[253]

Big shift. Before 1937, it was very difficult to get a divorce in Britain. You had to prove that your partner had committed adultery, and that was not an easy thing to do. With the Matrimonial Causes Act of 1937, new grounds, or 'offences', were introduced: cruelty, desertion, insanity or a long imprisonment. In the Divorce Reform Act of 1969, it became even easier to get a divorce. The "irretrievable breakdown" of a marriage was legally recognised.

The same year, "no fault" divorce was legalised in California, and was soon adopted across the US. In Canada, the legal term is "uncontested divorce." (There is currently a lawyer's web site called EZdivorce.ca, a name which really doesn't work in Canada, because the last letter of the alphabet is pronounced ZED, not ZEE like the Americans do.)

All of these legal terms — irretrievable breakdown, no fault, uncontested — are a recognition that a marriage breakdown is a very painful, very complicated, very messy affair. Legally proving adultery, proving cruelty, proving neglect is a tangled, ugly process. If a couple could agree that the 'marriage is over,' then there was no need for lengthy, expensive and ugly court battles. If it's uncontested, it's an EZdivorce — easy.

———•———

In terms of the Scriptures, there were three traditional grounds for divorce in the Old Testament: infertility — the inability to bear children;[254] sexual unfaithfulness — adultery;[255] and neglect — specifically of food, clothing and conjugal love.[256] Proving adultery or neglect was no easier in Bible times than it is today. It was just as painful, just as complicated, just as messy. And there was the same sort of divorce law devolution in the Jewish and Roman world over two thousand years ago. It is the social and religious context for passages like Mark's account of the Pharisees' attempt at trapping Jesus with what sounds like the straightforward question, "Is it lawful for a man to divorce his wife?"[257] It is the social and religious context for what sounds like the straightforward answer Jesus gave: "A man who divorces his wife and marries another commits adultery."[258] Similarly, it's the context for the Apostle Paul's admonition, "a husband must not divorce his wife."[259]

That devolution was based on Deuteronomy 24.1: there was the recognition that marriage can get so bad that if a man finds "something offensive," if his wife "becomes displeasing," then he could divorce her. This was the verse that the Pharisees quoted when they came to trap Jesus with their questions about divorce: "Is it lawful for a man to divorce his wife for *any and every reason*?"[260] For something offensive. If she becomes displeasing. If that passage is put in its context, the particular divorce the Pharisees had in mind was King Herod's. He certainly found something offensive in his first wife because he was lusting after Herodias, his brother's wife.

A group of Jewish lawyers called Hillelites, under the head Rabbi Hillel, instituted a "no fault" basis for divorce based on the wording of the phrase in Deuteronomy 24.1. The verse is translated various ways: "If a man marries a woman who becomes displeasing to him because he finds something indecent about her, he can write her a certificate of divorce."[261] "...if she does not win his favour because he finds something offensive in her..."[262] "...if she does not please him because he has found something offensive in her...."[263]

Hillel insisted that the words translated as something offensive, or something indecent could not be referring to sexual infidelity, because the punishment for adultery was death, not divorce.[264] Hillel insisted: "Anything which caused annoyance or embarrassment to a husband was a legitimate ground for divorce."[265] Husbands — have you ever been annoyed at your wife? Have you ever been embarrassed by her behaviour? Ladies? Ever annoyed or embarrassed with your hub? The Hillelites would say that you, like King Herod, have legitimate grounds for divorce.

Archaeologists have discovered written records from the First Century that document how lax this 'for any and every reason, divorce-on-demand' had become. No judge or court was involved. All a man had to do was write out a bill of divorce, date it, and deliver it to his wife in the presence of two witnesses. Throwing it at her in a fit of rage even counted as legitimate delivery![266] One man divorced his wife because she was a lousy cook. She kept burning his supper. Apparently, that both annoyed and embarrassed him.

Further, divorce 'for any and every reason' is the legal backstory that preceded the birth of Jesus. In Jewish tradition, betrothal — engagement — was a legally binding contract. In it, a couple pledged and promised sexual faithfulness and support, each to the other. Mary and Joseph were betrothed — legally engaged — and he discovered that she was pregnant. She maintained it was by the Holy Spirit. The text reads, "Joseph was a righteous man and *did not want to expose her to public disgrace,*" so he decided to *"divorce her quietly."*[267]

He could have divorced Mary on the grounds of her adultery, but that would have exposed her to public disgrace. It would be a painful, complicated, and messy affair, especially given that she was insistent that the Holy Spirit was the father. Instead, he decided to keep things quiet, and use the 'for any and every reason' option. He could simply say that she displeased him, that he found her offensive, and that would be the legal end of their engagement, an easy divorce. He wouldn't have to shame her by proving her adultery in a public trial.

Thirty-some years later, in contrast to Hillel's "annoyance" and "embarrassment," Jesus cited "the hardness of heart," alternatively translated as "stubbornness," as the only legitimate grounds for divorce.[268] God divorced Israel for the same reason — a hardness of heart that stubbornly, chronically turned away from him, the legitimate grounds for divorce because of adultery and habitual neglect. But Kingdom marriage, as Jesus taught it, is a world apart from 'for any and every reason' divorces. They are illegitimate because they completely trivialise marriage.

————•————

Back to the phrase, *"A sixteen year old must not drink."* We know that it goes without saying: he must not drink *alcohol*. Similarly, *"A husband must not divorce his wife"* — it goes without saying — *"for any and every reason."* That's why those remarried after a 'for any and every reason' divorce are adulterers. Their first marriage isn't legitimately over. Just because a wife is a lousy cook doesn't mean the marriage is so broken it can't be redeemed. It may be annoying; it may be embarrassing, but unless she's trying to poison her husband, her cooking is not legitimate grounds to end the marriage.

It is a completely different matter if the husband is addicted to pornography. On his wedding day, he pledged his faithfulness to his bride. In that, he promised sexual exclusivity, the giving of himself to her 'and to no other.' His habitual pornographic indulgence is grievously defective consent, for he intentionally and chronically turns away from his wife. Similarly, if the wife habitually denies her husband sexual intimacy, she too intentionally and chronically turns away from her husband.

Physical and emotional abuse, unrepentant nagging, and

sexual unfaithfulness in its many forms all signal defective consent, and make for a toxic relationship. But defining what are the legitimate, or even permissible grounds for divorce is a return to Law, and something grossly short of the questions, 'Where's grace in this?' 'What is Jesus yet calling forth?' 'What does graced redemption look like in these circumstances?' These are intimate, relational questions, and the answers may well be different for each and every set of circumstances, or even be different for the same circumstances but for the different people involved.

God purposes that none "should perish."[269] But the nature of true love is such that it can be rejected. Love can be refused. Jesus "came to his own, and his own people would not accept him."[270] Right across the board, hardness of heart forfeits redeeming grace. And just as hell is for those who perpetually insist on turning away from God's eternal love, so divorce is for those who stubbornly and habitually turn away from their spouse. The opposite is also true, both in relationship with Jesus, and with one's partner. Turning towards the other opens the heart; it accepts and appropriates the gift that is offered. "To all who did accept him… he gave the right to become children of God."[271]

Love conquers, but not by force. Jesus made this explicit when he stood accused before the Roman governor, Pilate. He said, "My kingdom does not belong to this world. If it did, my followers would be fighting to save me."[272] The power of true love is invitational. It does not, it cannot be dictated. To love and be loved is a choice. To love and be loved is an act of ongoing consent.

Notes

253. I am indebted to David Instone-Brewer for this illustration. *Divorce and Remarriage in the Bible*, Eerdmans, 2002.
254. Based on Genesis 1.22

255. Based on Deuteronomy 24.1

256. Based on Exodus 21.10

257. Mark 10.2

258. Luke 16.18

259. 1 Corinthians 7.11

260. Matthew 19.3, NIV.

261. NIV

262. REB

263. NET

264. Deuteronomy 22.20-21 and Leviticus 20.10

265. Rabbi Aquiba, one of Hillel's disciples, took things even further: a husband could divorce his wife if he "found someone else prettier than she." David Instone-Brewer, *Divorce and Remarriage*, Eerdmans, 2002, p.112.

266. Andrew Cornes, *Divorce and Remarriage*, Eerdmans, 1993, p. 181.

267. Matthew 1.19, NIV 1984, emphasis added.

268. Mark 10.5 and Matthew 19.8

269. See John 3.16

270. John 1.11

271. John 1.12

272. John 18.36

20
FROM ABOVE

———•———

Moving to Britain has had some 'lost in translation' moments. I'd travelled in the UK often enough to know the difference between trousers and pants, so I've been able to steer clear of that *faux pas*. Rucksacks and knapsacks didn't get me into any trouble, though fanny packs have. To date, it was a fancy dress birthday party that has posed the greatest difficulty. As period costumes were required, I went round to the local charity shops asking after vests. I got some special looks. (In retrospect, I get them quite often.) After a most unproductive afternoon of shopping, I learned that while I thought I was asking after waistcoats, it suddenly made sense why no one was selling used under-shirts.

———•———

Years ago, I was privileged to preach in Queensland Australia. One night is still particularly memorable. I was preaching on forgiveness: "If any of you has cause for complaint, you must forgive as the Lord forgave you."[273] In the course of the message, I asked a straightforward question: 'Whom do you want to deal with the wrong?'

Just before I was to leave the evening meeting, an elderly woman came up and leaned in close. She said, "I've never told anyone what I'm about to tell you." Her father was a doctor. When she was a young teenager, he got her pregnant. He performed her abortion. With tears that were ready to spill she asked, "How am I to forgive him as Christ has forgiven me?"

I gently took her hands. "I have no idea what I'm asking you to do, but I know it's right."

She just nodded. "I know too. But I don't know how...." We were both in tears as we slowly worked through the ravage she had endured.

For the balance of the conference, this woman's whole countenance was transformed. And when I returned to that church a year later, she was one of the first to come up and greet me. She looked ten years younger.

That evening left a profound imprint on my heart and spirit, and it began to open a whole new understanding of my life in Christ. I realised as never before that an essential of faith had been lost in translation.

Jesus said, "Very truly I tell you, no one can see the kingdom of God unless they are born again."[274] A good study Bible will have a little note explaining that the Greek phrase *genaethae anothen*, 'born again,' has a double meaning and can also be translated 'born from above.' This has often been misunderstood. In its context, Jesus was speaking to Nicodemus, and he misunderstood: "How can someone be born when they are old? Surely they cannot enter a second time into their mother's womb to be born!"[275] Jesus clarified: "What is born of the flesh is flesh, and what is born of the Spirit is spirit." And then he repeated himself: "You must all be born *anothen* — from above."[276]

There's a contrast here that mustn't be lost in translation. Back up a bit. By way of introduction, Jesus said to Nathanael and the others who had gathered, "In very truth I tell you all: you will see heaven wide open and God's angels ascending and descending upon the Son of Man."[277] A short while later Jesus said, "He who comes from above is above all others; he who is from the earth belongs to the earth and uses earthly speech. He who comes from heaven bears witness to what he has seen and heard."[278] To the Pharisees Jesus said, "I know where I come from, and where I am going.... You judge by worldly standards.... You belong to this world below, I to the world above."[279] Add to all of this the way the Apostle John concluded the prologue to his Gospel: "The law was given through Moses, but grace and truth came through Jesus Christ. No one has ever seen God; God's only Son, he who is nearest to the Father's heart, has made him known."[280]

Time after time, Jesus tried to make it clear that there are two realities: the natural and the spiritual; earth and heaven; the world below and the world above. If we are not "born from above," we are constrained to "judge according to the flesh;" "by human standards;" "by outward appearances."[281] Law rules when we live from below; grace, truth and the Father's heart are revealed when we live from above.

Back to Queensland Australia, and the sermon on forgiveness. Jesus said, "If you forgive others the wrong they have done, your heavenly Father will also forgive you; but if you do not forgive others, then your Father will not forgive the wrongs that you have done."[282] At face value, that sounds very conditional. Flip it: it doesn't sound at all like unconditional grace. But put it within the 'frame' of the teaching that's just been rehearsed. We cannot see the Kingdom of God unless we are born from above, and we choose where we want to live, either from above, or from below. I forget where I heard it, but it is staggeringly true: 'Nurturing unforgiveness is like eating rat poison, and expecting the rat to die.' Unforgiveness only breeds resentment, bitterness and retribution. We can live from below, with judgement, with what we deserve, giving to others what they deserve, or we can live from above, where mercy triumphs over judgement. And receiving mercy, we embrace mercy in our dealings with others. We choose: what's fair, or what's forgiven.

This one's an either/or, not a both/and. "Do not judge, and you will not be judged."[283] From above, God sees us through the corrective lens of mercy, and he extends to us unconditional forgiveness. If we don't see ourselves the same way, if we don't find ourselves in his mercy, if we insist on living from below, passing judgement on others, and nurturing grudges and resentment, then we place ourselves under the judgement of God, a position he has chosen not to see us from. But he honours our choice. And he counts it the choice of choices. We can find ourselves in the unconditional, superabundant, unmerited mercy extended to us in the unfailing love of Jesus, or we can insist that we only want what's fair, what's deserved, what's earned. But we can't ride two horses at the same time. The 'freely you've received, freely give'[284] principle applies here. As we've received unconditional forgiveness, we are to give that same unconditional forgiveness to those who have wronged us. Recall the distinction made between image and likeness.[285] While we are all made in the image of God the question is, do we bear any likeness? That we are made in the image means we have the potential for life in God; bearing the likeness of God means we have realised something of that potential. That's where we all live out life, in between image and likeness, potential and realisation. God is forgiving; are we? There is a serious lack of spiritual congruity if we wilfully try to live both from above and from below at the same time — receiving heaven's forgiveness for our failures and wrongs, but not extending it to those who have failed and wronged us.

Living from above extends beyond forgiveness and judgement. Recall the parable of the Sower. From below, the focus is on the soil, and the question, 'Am I good enough?' From above, the Good News is that the seed, Jesus, yields supernatural harvest, even in the most deprived of conditions. Similarly, living from above changes the way we understand sin and restoration. From below, we find fault with ourselves, and with others. We live under condemnation, and find fault with those around us. But from above, God sees us "accepted in the Beloved."[286] And knowing that there is, in Christ, no condemnation, we are to see ourselves, and others, the same way. From below, there's a measure of unsettledness as I keep asking, 'Do I have enough faith?' From above, I can rest in Christ's unbounded faithfulness. Again and again, this is why 'We lift our hearts to the Lord.'

A romp through the Apostle John's writings helps to anchor all of this. "God so loved the world that he gave...."[287] From 'above,' this is love 'come down.' In Greek, the word translated 'love' is *agape*. It is the same word that John used of Jesus' love: "He had always loved his own who were in the world, and he loved them to the end."[288] Jesus loved with perfect congruence, just as God the Father loves. The word *agape* is used again when Jesus said, "As the Father has loved me, so I have loved you. Dwell in my love."[289] Here, congruence, image and likeness are extended beyond Jesus, to us as his followers.

The Apostle John personally received and appropriated that love, for he repeatedly called himself "the disciple whom Jesus loved."[290] And it is this same self-understanding that John extended to the church, for we share "a common life" with the Father and his Son Jesus Christ.[291] Thereafter, John addressed those to whom he wrote as *agapatoi*, the collective noun form of *agape*. The KJV and the NASB preserve a literal translation, rendering it "Beloved." To diminish *agapatoi* to "Dear friends"[292] is to miss the congruence John purposed.

In the middle of his letter John said, "Consider how great is the love which the Father has bestowed on us in calling us his children!"[293] and time and again he insisted, "*Agapatoi*, let us *agape* one another, for *agape* is from God"[294] "Beloved, if God so loved us, we also ought to love one another."[295] "We love, because he first loved us."[296]

Further, John took great pains to call the beloved beyond their incongruence: "God is light.... If we say that we have fellowship with him and yet walk in the darkness, we lie and do not practice the truth."[297] "Whoever claims to love God yet hates his brother or sister is a liar. For whoever does not love their brother or sister, whom they have seen, cannot love God, whom they have not seen."[298]

Though he didn't use the terms 'from above' and 'from below,' the great Danish theologian Søren Kierkegaard nonetheless explained things this way:

> Take a purely human relationship. If the lover is not able to speak the beloved's language, he or she must learn it, however difficult it may seem to them — otherwise, if they cannot talk together, there cannot be a happy relationship. It is the same with dying to the world in order to be able to love God. God is Spirit — only one who has died to the world can speak this language at all. If you do not wish to die to the world, then you cannot love God either; you are talking about entirely different matters than he is.[299]

In a consideration of love, dying to the world may sound morbid. Death is, however, the ultimate end of life from below. Resurrection only comes from above. And, paradoxically, "unless a grain of wheat falls into the ground and dies, it remains that and nothing more; but if it dies, it bears a rich harvest."[300] We are invited to learn and to speak the Beloved's language, and that has us talking about entirely different matters than we would if we were still living from below.

Notes

273. Colossians 3.12
274. John 3.3, NIV.
275. John 3.4, NIV.
276. John 3.6-7, NET. See also Peterson's paraphrase in *The Message*.
277. John 1.51
277. John 3.31. The word translated "above" is from the same Greek word in John 3.3, *anothen*.
279. John 8.14-15; 23
280. John 1.17-18
281. John 8.15, NASB, NIV, NET.
282. Matthew 6.14-15
283. Matthew 7.1
284. See Matthew 10.8, NIV.
285. Genesis 1.26
286. KJV; see NASB.
287. John 3.16
288. John 13.1
289. John 15.9
290. John 13.23; 19.26; 21.7; 21.20
291. See 1 John 1.3 and 7
292. NIV, REB, NET, GNB, NLT.
293. 1 John 3.1
294. 1 John 4.7, NASB.
295. 1 John 4.11, NASB.
296. 1 John 4.19, NASB.
297. 1 John 1.5-6, NASB.
298. 1 John 4.17, NIV.
299. *Journals and Papers*. Vol. 1, Journal entry 538 [1852] Edited and translated by Howard V. Hong and Edna H. Hong, Bloomington: Indiana University Press, 1967, p. 219.
300. John 12.24

21
LIFE'S MYSTERIES

—•—

I'm fascinated with words, and even more fascinated when they just don't make sense. For instance, why is 'abbreviation' such a long word? Why is there only one word for 'thesaurus'? Why are there five syllables in the word 'monosyllabic'?

It's not just words that don't make sense. How come there's only one Monopolies Commission? Why do banks charge you a non-sufficient funds fee on money they already know you don't have? And why do they call it the Department of Interior when they're in charge of everything outdoors?

Then there's life's mysteries. If they can make the black box survive the worst of airplane crashes, why don't they make the whole plane from that same stuff? Why does sour cream have an expiration date? And, if they put pictures of missing children on milk cartons, why don't they put pictures of missing husbands on beer cans?

Mysteries, shrouded in enigmas, wrapped in conundrums. Rather like a passage in the Book of Acts. The Apostle Paul was in Thessalonica for three weeks, meeting in the synagogue for three Sabbaths and, as was often the case with his ministry, both a revival and a riot broke out. He had to leave in haste and there's no record of his return. Yet a thriving church was planted.[301] Paul wrote to that little gathering of believers at least twice — our New Testament letters of 1st and 2nd Thessalonians — and Paul said of this young church, "You have become a model for all believers in Macedonia and in Achaia; from you the word of the Lord rang out... and everywhere your faith in God has become common knowledge."[302] After just three weeks of ministry!

We're not given any detail or explanation but that Paul went to the synagogue and taught the Scriptures over three Sabbaths. A man named Jason is mentioned, though we're not told anything about him. He's given no introduction, and there's no context for his sudden arrival on the scene. All we know is that the resident Jews weren't at all happy with the numbers that turned to Jesus. They recruited the local skinheads and made for Jason's house, ready to rumble. Anticipating a riot, Paul and Silas quickly left town; disappointed, the mob dragged Jason before the local magistrates and caused him such grief that he had to post bond before they would let him go. And that's all we're told.

Thereafter, we can only make conjectures, based on the fact that Jason hosted Paul and Silas over their three weeks of ministry. Jason presumably was one of the first Thessalonian converts. He presumably opened not only his home but also his heart and spirit. There's enough there to know that Jason was one who showed kindness to Paul. And kindness works miracles.

———•———

As a travelling itinerant preacher, I've stayed in a lot of different homes. Most of the time my hosts are very pleasant, gracious people with a guest bed and something of the gift of hospitality. Once in a while, my hosts have been a different breed. They've had an uncommon spiritual passion for Jesus. Like a cat hanging on a screen door, they won't let go. We go back to their house after the evening meeting, and they've got questions. Really good questions. They open their spirits, and open their hearts. There's a vulnerability, a teachability, a receptivity that means that things go really deep really fast. We've studied the Scriptures together. We've prayed together. I've often stayed up into the wee hours with folks like that. There's the sense that Kingdom seed is being planted, and as Jesus said in the parable of the sower, that seed will produce thirty, sixty, a hundred fold. I've often thought that however good the conference might have been, there's the sense that the Lord sent me to the place just for those late-night times with my hosts.

Might it have been that Jason was one of those types? Paul didn't name him in his letters to the Thessalonians. There are no greetings, either at the start or close of the letters as he often does, as in Romans 16 for instance: "Greetings from Gaius, my host, and from Erastus, and our brother Quartus…" But if Jason was that kind of a guy — open, receptive, surrendered, obedient, passionate about Jesus and the work of his Kingdom — might Paul have been thinking about him as he wrote:

> Grace to you and peace. We always thank God for you all, and mention you in our prayers. We continually call to mind, before our God and Father, how your faith has shown itself in action, your love in labour, and your hope of our Lord Jesus Christ in perseverance.[303]

Just like Jason, very few would know anything about Elizabeth Anne Everest. (She's no relation to the mountain.) Elizabeth was a nanny in Victorian England. She died in near obscurity, in 1895. Twenty years earlier, she assumed the care of a child whom the boy's mother complained was a difficult child to manage. That assessment was understated. The boy kicked, he screamed, and he bullied. The word 'monster' was often used of him.

It was not solely the young boy's fault. These were the days when 'Children were to be seen but not heard.' This boy's parents outdistanced many of their fellow aristocratic Victorians. Quite to the neglect of their son, his parents gave themselves to their political careers and social ambitions. One biographer nuanced their controlling interests: "Both his parents were famous for sex." His father died of syphilis, and it was rumoured that his mother had over two hundred lovers. Not untypical for the era, the child was sent to boarding school at age seven. His letters home had a consistent theme: "Please do do do do do do come down to see me…. I have been so disappointed so many times about your coming." These were not just the longings of a homesick little boy. There was "constant hoping for visits that did not take place." The parents very rarely visited. And when he was home from school, the boy's father thought he was retarded and seldom spoke to him. When his father did have contact it was to vent his volcanic rage on the child. More than one historian concluded that the man loathed his son.

Not surprisingly, the child did poorly at school. One of his early report cards reads: "Composition — feeble. Writing — good, but terribly slow. Spelling — about as bad as it can be. Diligence — does not quite understand the meaning of hard work — must make up his mind to do so next term." Remarks from his Headmaster were similar: "Very bad — is a constant trouble to everybody and is always in some scrape or other. He cannot be trusted to behave himself anywhere. He has no ambition." The boy was so afraid of failing his father's expectations, he suffered from extreme anxiety, shaking, sweating and nausea before his exams. He developed both a lisp and a stammer, and regularly had the lowest marks in many of his classes. Though his father was a graduate of Oxford, neither he nor anyone else had any expectations that the boy was destined for university. His grades were so poor, three attempts were required before he squeezed into military college.

It was upon this child that Elizabeth Ann Everest concentrated her affection. Everest was a Christian, and she devoted herself to the nurture and formation of the young life that was entrusted to her care. She became the primary influence and the relational centre in the troubled boy's life.

His name? Winston Leonard Spencer Churchill, the future Prime Minister of England, and leader of the Allied Forces during the Second World War.[304] Of Everest, Churchill wrote, "She is in my mind associated more than anything else with home.... She is more fond of me and my brother than any other person in the world. I shall never know such a friend again."[305] Violet Asquith, one of Churchill's closest female friends, paid her this tribute: "In Winston's solitary childhood and unhappy school days, Mrs. Everest was his comforter, his strength and stay, his one source of unfailing human understanding. She was the fireside at which he dried his tears and warmed his heart. She was the night light by his bed. She was his security."

In the dark days of the 1930s the military machinery of the Third Reich began to grind Europe to pieces. Other leaders of his age vacillated and negotiated the easy road of political compromise and appeasement. Churchill rose to the occasion, and defined the crisis of the time in the stark Christian terms that moved the Allied world to greatness. One biographer wrote: "Behind the arsenal of his words, behind the artillery of his vision, was the simple teaching of a devoted nanny who served her God by investing in the destiny of a troubled boy."

When Churchill died in 1965 at the age of ninety, the *Daily*

Express named him "the mightiest man, surely, in all the wondrous history of England." Isaiah Berlin called him "the largest human being of our times."[306] There was one framed picture on the stand beside his deathbed, a photograph of 'Woom,' his beloved nanny. She had died seventy years before. Churchill biographer, Boris Johnson, paid Everest this tribute: "It is hard to know exactly how much the world owes Winston Churchill's nanny. But if anyone taught him to be good and kind and by and large truthful, it was surely her. She it was, I reckon, who helped him to that vast and generous moral sense."[307] One can only wonder what would have happened to Churchill without her influence upon his life.

———•———

Life is full of mysteries. But this we know: of all things, love conquers. When we come under another's judgment, it causes us to shut down, to withdraw, to try to protect ourselves. Love does just the opposite, and then some: its influence can open us up, call us out, and call forth the best in us.

I recognise that there is something in us that likes things simple, and that judgmental 'black and white' categories are easier to manage than relational 'shades of grey.' Complexity, ambiguity, and uncertainty unsettle most of us. I understand. So let me finish with a few final questions.

Who is it that gets to say which verses of Scripture need to be taken literally? And why is it that the uncomplicated imperative, "Do not judge" isn't one of them? What might church look like if we took literally that wonderful declaration, "Mercy triumphs over judgment."[308] What if that became our relational 'black and white'? That whatever the issue, whatever the problem, whatever the circumstances, our first question was, 'Where's grace in this?' What if we kept things simple, and in God's name, by God's Spirit, we were excessively kind to those who were falling short? What if in God's name, by God's Spirit, we were excessively gentle with those who made a mess of things?

I know, I know: 'What about accountability? What about consequences? What about tough love?' They have their place, and they have their time, but they ought not to be our first response. Or our seventh. Or our seventieth.[309] How repeatedly kind has God been to us in our particular failing? How repeatedly patient has God been to you in your particular failings? With all that we've worked through over the course of this book, hear again the Apostle Paul's question: "Do you despise his wealth of kindness and tolerance and patience, failing to see that God's kindness is meant to lead you to repentance?"[310] Might it be time to change the way we think?

Unto the renewing of our minds,[311] there are several prayers in the letters to the Thessalonians. I commend them to you.

May the Lord make your love increase and overflow to one another and to everyone…. May He make your hearts firm, so that you may stand before our God and Father holy and faultless when our Lord Jesus comes…. May the Lord direct your heart towards the love of God and the steadfastness of Christ."[312]

Notes

301. Acts 17.1 ff.
302. 1 Thessalonians 1.7-8
303. 1 Thessalonians 1.2-3
304. The sources for the preceding quotations are as follows: Boris Johnson, *The Churchill Factor: How One Man Made History*. Hodder and Stoughton, 2015, p.51; *The Churchills: A Family at the Heart of History*, Mary Lovell, Little, Brown: London, 2011, pgs.580 and x; *Churchill*, Ashley Jackson. Quercus: London, 2012, p.33; *Churchill*, Roy Jenkins. Pan Books: London, 2002, p.9; *Jennie Churchill*, Anne Sebba. John Murray, 2007, p.129; *The Churchills*, p.68.
305. *The Churchills*, Lovell, p.117.

306. *Man of the Century: Winston Churchill*, John Ramsden. HarperCollins, London, 2002, p. 138.
307. *The Churchill Factor*, p.115.
308. James 2.13
309. See Matthew 18.22
310. Romans 2.4
311. Romans 12.2
312. 1 Thessalonians 3.12-13; 2 Thessalonians 3.5